Modern Retouching Manual

Modern Retouching Manual

2nd Edition

by
Kitty West

AMPHOTO
American Photographic Book Publishing Co., Inc.
GARDEN CITY, NEW YORK

Third Printing, February 1979

2nd EDITION

Published in Garden City, N.Y., by American Photographic Book Publishing Company, Inc. Manufactured in the United States of America.

Library of Congress Catalog Card No. 72-75556
ISBN 0-8174-0508-9

Contents

PART II COLOR

INTRODUCTION

What Is Retouching?

In photography, declares Noah Webster, retouching means "to improve, as a negative, by removing imperfections and giving a fine finish."

The groundwork for retouching was laid when the Swiss painter and photographer Isenring attempted to improve highlights on some daguerreotype portraits, about the year 1841. Actually, the Viennese photographer Emil Rabending (1823–86) invented retouching. The work was done with graphites (practically the same as are used today) on glass negatives, and replaced the practice of correcting positive prints. The art of retouching is now over one hundred years old; from the very beginning it has been an important part of photography. The reasons are simple. As long as photography produces an image on film, glass, paper, or some other substance that can be damaged, and as long as that image may be improved, retouching is a necessary expedient.

Although unbelievable strides in the modernization of photo equipment, lighting, and laboratory procedure have been made, neither the human face nor the basic approach to retouching it has changed. Today's photography business is more in need of retouchers than ever before. Whereas formerly the photographer's main income was derived from salon portraiture, today the photographer is swamped with school orders, and needs retouchers to work on negatives of smiling, grinning youngsters who have freckles, pimples, bony shoulders, hairdos that need smoothing, and other flaws in need of correction.

To the average customer the word "retoucher" symbolizes someone who will perform all requested corrections with a magic wand. He knows nothing about the technique and cares less. If the picture falls short of the anticipated result, the retoucher is usually blamed.

There is an anecdote that indicates how little the public knows about photo retouching or restoration. To prove the point, here is the joke, as old as the hills, but still appropriate.

A lady enters a photo studio clutching an old wilted photograph of her deceased husband. She inquires of the photographer if a good enlargement of the little picture can be made. He assures her that it can be done. Then she asks if the crossed eyes can be fixed, and the bow tie changed into a long one. The photographer assures her that these changes can be made. She keeps requesting more changes. Finally she points to the dated straw hat in the picture.

"Can you even remove the hat and show his wavy hair?"

"We can fix that too," promises the exasperated proprietor of the studio.

After discussing price and other details of the order, the lady leaves. Just as she reaches the doorway, the photographer calls after her: "Madam, when we remove the hat, on which side shall we part the hair?"

The lady turns around and replies indignantly: "Remove the hat and you'll see where!"

Since I have been a professional retoucher and instructor for many years, the reader will understand that my statements and advice on retouching techniques presented in this book are based on long practical experience in this field.

Although the fate of a picture rests with the operation of the camera, it is indisputable that the final polish that makes the rough diamond saleable rests in the hands of the competent retoucher.

Photo retouching is more than just dabbing a few strokes on blemishes and wrinkles and hoping they will not show up on the enlarged print. Just as a doctor is able to look at an X-ray and see what ails the patient, so the competent retoucher sees more on the negative than the untrained viewer would. He will know what features to accentuate and what to subdue or take out altogether. He can tell what type of skin the person has, what lines are an indication of bad habits, and what facial imperfections have been caused by natural aging.

Retouching is a highly artistic profession, and most rewarding in every way for one who would like to see the human face reproduced to its fullest advantage. Retouching skills should not be limited only to retouchers. Anyone who likes photography well enough to make it his hobby or full-time occupation should know how to retouch his own negatives. If nature has not endowed a person sitting for a portrait with beautiful features, even the best photographer or lighting conditions cannot always improve him, but at least the photographer who knows retouching can disguise those elements that detract from the portrait, and keep the photograph from looking only like an enlarged snapshot.

Retouching is not only applicable to portrait photography. Once the retouching technique is mastered, it can be applied to every kind of correction on film. A line in the face or a crack in the wall requires about the same treatment with the retouching stroke.

In every phase of modern photography, whether it be landscape, commercial, exteriors, fashion, pictorial, etc., there is always room for picture improvement—heightening a detail here, eliminating a defect there—in order to achieve the finest possible result.

There is no secret touchstone, no royal road to success in

photo retouching. Three simple ingredients are essential: *negatives, time,* and *patience.* As in any handicraft, retouching requires good sight and a gift of observation. These ingredients are indeed simple, considering that they may enable one to earn a very satisfactory livelihood that is not limited by age or family circumstances.

If the fundamentals are learned correctly from the start, the beginner can easily achieve excellent results within a few weeks. Many have attempted to do retouching without previous instruction or knowledge, but have given up after a few hit-and-miss trials, feeling that mastery of the art would require months or years of practice and special artistic ability. This wrong conclusion should be corrected right now.

I must honestly say that retouching *cannot* be learned on your own, without at least some personally guided instruction in the beginning. Retouching can only be comprehended by visual demonstration, as anyone having tried it on his own from the first step knows. In this book I shall try to present every phase of work on negatives in a simple and easy-to-understand manner. The beginner can work directly on some of the sample illustrations in the practice section. Throughout the book he will find every possible facet or problem explained and the practical function of every tool of the trade discussed.

It is an incorrect assumption that in photo retouching long hours have to be spent in some dark corner. Retouching is a relaxing occupation. The eyes will seldom tire following the movement of the hand on a negative. In fact, this type of work is often soothing to nervous people. One is not likely to see a good retoucher flitting about. He sits calmly at his desk, relaxed and absorbed in his work.

The work of the average professional photographer has to do with photographing weddings, anniversaries, club members, babies, and school functions. These supply the lion's share of the profitable income for a studio. Once his customers are well-satisfied, they remain faithful to the photographer, and take their friends and families to him. No amount of advertising can keep a photographer in business for long. No "specials" or "give-away" enticements will help much. He has to deliver what the customer wants: a pleasing image of himself. In other words, a *retouched portrait.*

All explanations throughout this book are applicable to the amateur photographer as well as to the professional. Anyone handling a camera and film should know how to do corrective work on negatives. Through the medium of retouching, the amateur photographer can achieve the perfection of a professional.

The usual procedure of resorting to tedious spotting and bleaching with chemicals can be eliminated by the substitution of good retouching. Efforts that consume hours and require great patience can be reduced, because satisfactory results can be achieved within minutes by work on the negative. Retouching can produce pleasing results even on delicate filmpack.

Perfecting himself in this occupation is up to the reader. Once the initial difficulties (which confront us in everything new) are overcome, much pleasure and monetary compensation can be derived from retouching. One may even regret that this skill was not acquired sooner.

The goal of a retoucher, or better still, the guiding motto, should be: *retouching must be executed in such a manner that the picture never reveals or allows the observer to guess that corrections have been made.* Only then is the retoucher's artistry successful.

One important factor not even the best book or instructor can pass on: the will and determination to succeed. As an ancient Greek poet said:

BEFORE THE GATES OF EXCELLENCE
THE HIGH GODS HAVE PLACED SWEAT.
LONG IS THE ROAD THERETO AND STEEP
AND ROUGH AT FIRST,
BUT WHEN THE HEIGHT IS WON,
THEN IS THERE EASE.

PART I

Black and White

CHAPTER 1

General Information on Negatives and Retouching Pencils

"Reading" the Negative

Although the experienced retoucher must be able to cope with all sizes and qualities of film, it is vitally important that the beginner do his practice work on "normal" negatives. In photographic terms a "normal" or "average" negative is one that, when viewed against the light, will have a soft gray tone throughout, even in the shadow areas.

The dictionary definition of the word "negative" is this: "In photography, a photographic picture on glass, film, etc., in which the lights and shades are the opposite of those in nature." The negative is used as a plate from which to print positive impressions on paper or some other material. Its highlights are quite opaque (dense) and it descends by delicate gradations to its deepest shadows, which should be represented by clear glass or film. Thus the handicap the beginner must overcome is the difficulty of "reading" a negative: seeing the positive in reverse. He must look upon a negative as though it were a positive, and familiarize himself with the reversed image not merely in black-and-white tones but also in terms of the actual change in appearance that will occur when the film is printed. For instance, if a sitter is facing toward the right on the negative he will face to the left on the positive. Only when the negative is on the retouching stand with the shiny side up will the image be in the same position as in the final print—but we shall come to this later.

If the beginner is working on a face, he will have no difficulty in recognizing blotches, specks, and strong lines on the negatives. These appear much lighter than the rest of the recorded density and are ideal for initial practice retouching.

All other portions of the face that are represented in halftones and shadows should be left alone until the basic stroke technique is acquired and the retoucher learns to "read" a negative. Actually, this is rather like learning to spell; a child must learn the alphabet before he can form letters into words. A musician must learn the keyboard before he can play a tune. So must the retoucher learn strokes and a light touch before he can achieve a modeled, or artistic, effect on a negative.

In a short time the retoucher's eyes become accustomed to the fine variations in the negative gray; and with practice he will be able to create the modeled effect so desirable in high-grade portraiture. The secret of this effect lies in the way the retoucher conforms his strokes to the facial planes. Highlights and soft tones should be in the right places, and densities should be blended into contour for a feeling of depth and naturalness.

Types of Negatives

Before we concern ourselves with questions of technique, however, we should learn to recognize each of the following types of negative density:

1. *The thin negative* is transparent throughout and comparable to a silk fabric. This type is not too difficult to retouch as long as a harder pencil is used and some experience in retouching has been gained. Retouching should be kept to a minimum to preserve the softness of the picture.

2. *The medium, or normal, negative* can be compared to a cotton material. It has a variation of gray tones, the highlights appearing rather pronounced and the shadows a soft, translucent gray. This is the most desirable for retouching and the best practice negative.

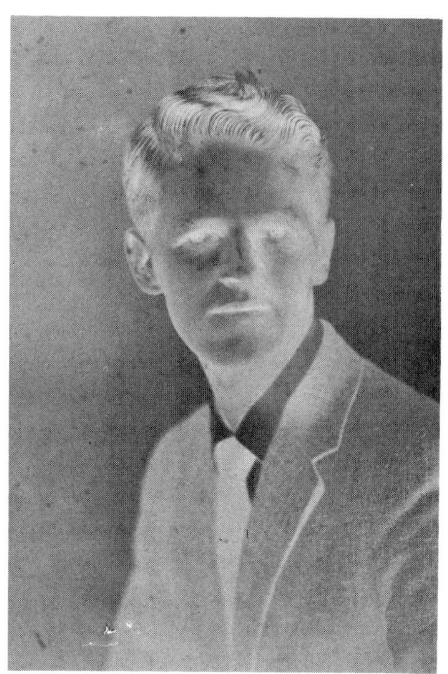

Fig. 1. Thin negative.

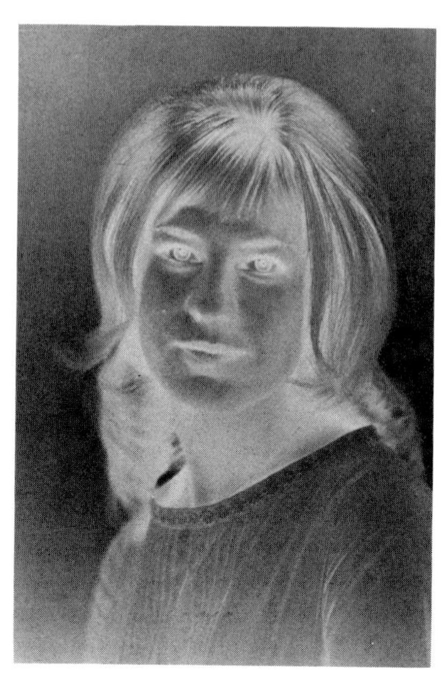

Fig. 2. Normal negative.

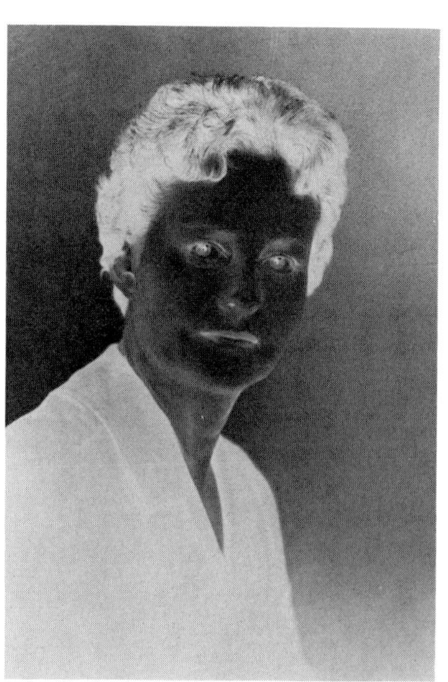

Fig. 3. Dense negative.

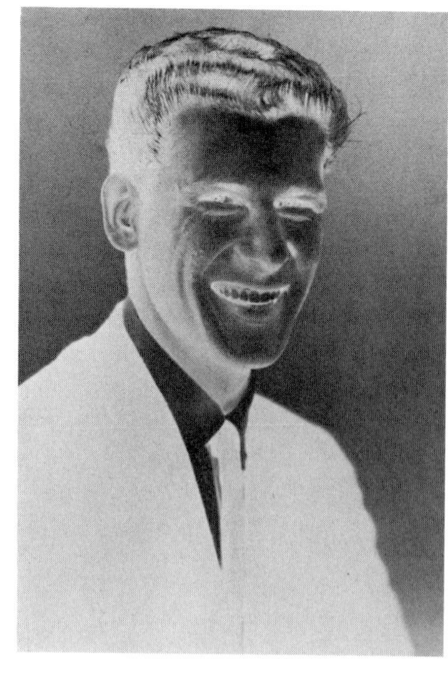

Fig. 4. Negative with strong contrast.

3. The dense negative will appear dark to our eyes and can be compared to a thick material such as wool. Accordingly, a soft pencil will leave more deposit of graphite on the film and match the dark tone of the emulsion.

4. The "contrasty" negative is the most difficult of the group to retouch. It has strong layers of emulsion in the highlights and abruptly dips into deep shadows, appearing absolutely clear and devoid of gray tone. Purposely-made contrasty negatives are very artistic for character studies or low-key portraiture, or pictures in a somber mood. They are also often the result of outdoor portraiture, where strong sunlight was the light source. Retouching on contrasty negatives must be done very intelligently, and it is advisable to leave such negatives alone until retouching with dye and pencil has been mastered. A retoucher can make or break a portrait of this kind.

Figures 1–4 are negative reproductions that illustrate several of the most common types of negatives. The difference in their quality is quite obvious. The retoucher must learn to choose the right pencils to match the density of each particular negative. (See page 30.)

The Pencil: Mending Medium

The silver deposit on film resembles a texture. Shadows and other transparent areas, such as lines and blemishes, are not covered with the silver deposit, and if greatly magnified would appear as tiny vales and depressions on the emulsion. The heavier the deposit of silver, the greater the contrast of lines and shadows indicated on the image. Since we are comparing the film surface to a texture or material on which we work, we have to consider the retouching pencil as a *mending medium* that covers or pulls the torn and uneven texture together to render a clean skin surface. The retoucher deposits, or better yet, injects the graphite of the lead pencil *into* the fine lines or blotches of the negative. This requires an accurate touch, the coordination of eye and hand that must be learned correctly from the beginning.

Pencils are the retoucher's primary tools and as such must be kept in first-class condition to render good service. Just as one cannot sew with a broken needle or paint with a frayed brush, so one cannot retouch with a dull pencil point.

Each retouching pencil matches one of the tones of the negative gray, and the student of retouching will soon learn to discern the characteristic quality of each hardness.

In the following chapter we shall discuss the retouching pencil and its use in greater detail.

CHAPTER 2

Retouching Equipment

The tools of the retoucher are inexpensive, and a few items, such as retouching stand, magnifying glass, or pencil holders, can last a lifetime (Fig. 5). Each item and its use will be explained as we progress. For both professional and amateur retouchers the following items comprise all equipment necessary:

1. Retouching stand
2. Retouching leads with holders (Never regular pencils!)
3. Sable brushes Nos. 00 and 000
4. Bottle of retouching medium ("dope")
5. K. West retouching dye
6. Etching knife (see Chapter 6, "Etching")
7. Envelope with fine sandpaper
8. Magnifying glass
9. Printing frame for outdoor proofing
10. Proofing paper
11. (Choice of opaque, dyes, or new color negative dyes, if necessary)

A small tool box will hold the utensils neatly, and if treated with care and kept meticulously clean, the equipment need not be replenished for a long time.

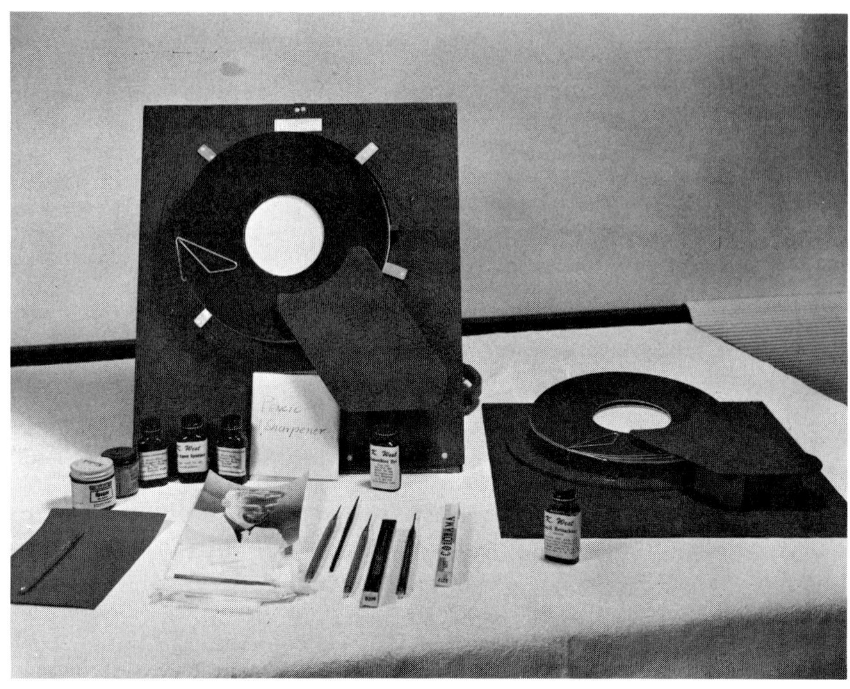

Fig. 5. Retouching equipment. Patented retouching device on folding stand. Patented device alone (right) can attach to ordinary frame. K. West dyes, pencil holders with graphites and color leads, Ideal etching knife with honing paper may be obtained from the National Retouchers Guild.

General Information on Retouching Stands

In my many years of association with photographers one particular thing has puzzled me. Hundreds of dollars are invested in cameras, lights, darkroom equipment, and countless modern innovations, but the retouching desk and stand remain in most instances crudely-constructed objects resembling a torture apparatus more than anything else. They are certainly a far cry from what they ought to be. When in a matter of an hour the hands feel numb, the eyes smart, and the back begins to hurt, it is easy to see how retouching can become a dreaded task.

To a retoucher the stand is the most important part of his trade, something that should be constructed with great care. It is not often taken into consideration that sometimes the wrong angle of the slanted board, the incorrect distance of the light behind the stand, or an improper rest area for the hand can make a world of difference to someone who spends many hours a day at this task. Naturally, anyone who works constantly in a sitting position needs relaxation from time to time, so the retoucher should make it a habit to get up from work every half hour, stretch his arms, walk around the room, take a few deep breaths of *outside* air, and return refreshed to his desk. Also, frequent blinking while working is highly recommended.

During the many years I have been an instructor of retouching, prospective students have often brought me home-constructed retouching stands for inspection and approval. Either they already had one in their studio or some friend had parted with it because he had given up retouching. Whenever I saw the stand I knew the reason why the previous owner had gladly parted with the contraption!

Retouching stands are generally not sold by camera stores, and only one or two brand names are sold by the companies themselves. Also, the trade is not so brisk, because a retouching stand does not undergo the changes of other studio equipment and thus remains a "stepchild" of the photographic trade.

Usually a carpenter or handy photographer constructs a box with an opening, puts a light behind it—and presto!—the stand is made. But there is more to the construction of a good retouching stand than one might think. A ready-made stand is in the end still the best investment. When you total the cost in time and money of the home-constructed stand—the necessary tools, the varnish, plexiglass or opal glass, lumber, cutting, hinges and screws—the investment is almost as great as the cost of the ready-made stand.

BUYING A STAND

When buying any ready-made retouching stand, look out

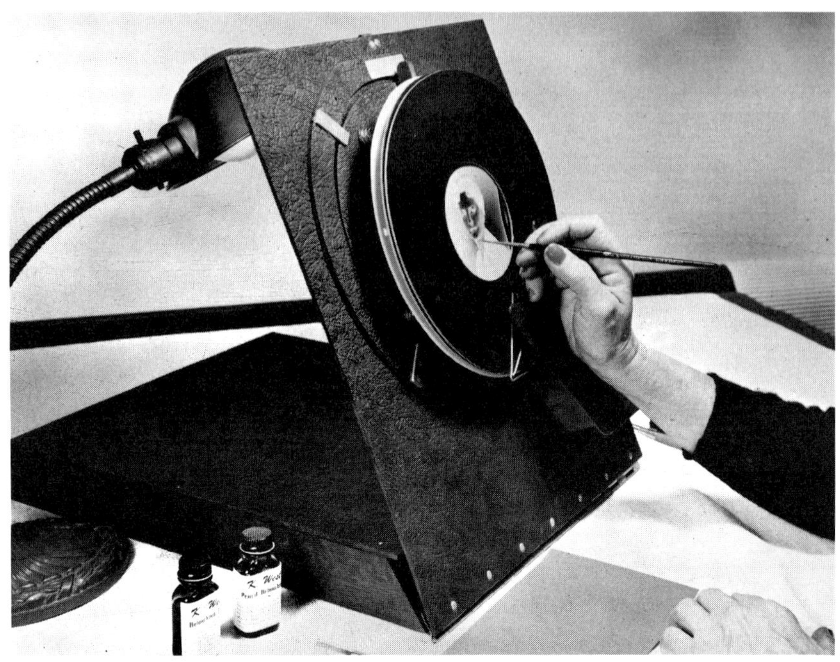

Fig. 6. Correct slant of retouching stand. Retoucher's wrist should lean on handrest. Pencil or brush should be held at a right angle, like a dart aiming toward area to be retouched.

Fig. 7 (Below, left). Side view of closed K. West retouching stand. Fig. 8 (Below, right). The advantage of the Patent device is the adjustable mask that can hold any size roll film.

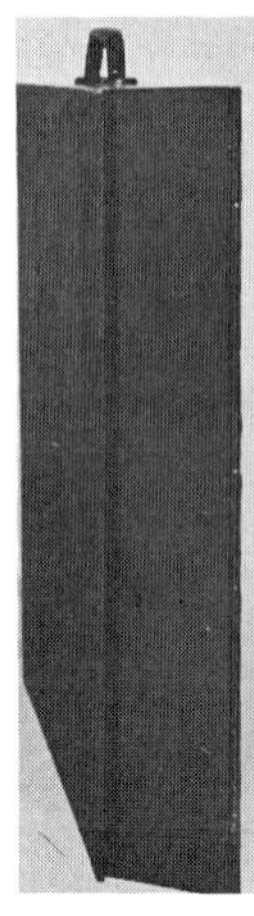

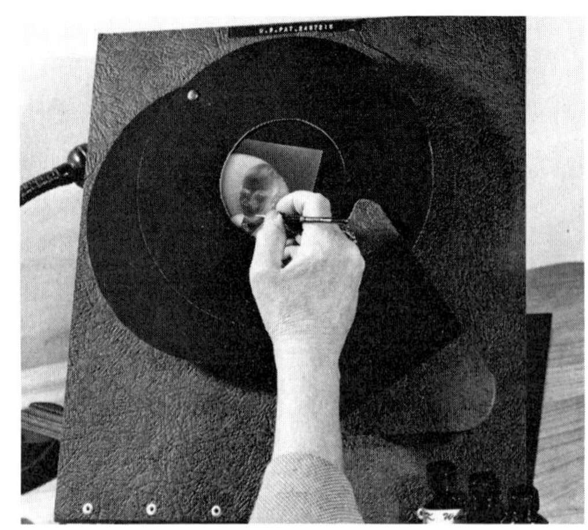

for certain disadvantages. The light bulb should not be attached directly to the board. If the electric bulb is too near the opal glass or plexiglass on which the negative is placed, the glass warms up and will eventually warp or curl the film. Furthermore, a strong glare causes eye strain. The most practical illumination is a small gooseneck lamp with a 75-watt or 100-watt *blue frosted* bulb that can be adjusted and moved back-and-forth as the negative density requires. Most hardware stores carry a full line of these special bulbs. Markets very seldom carry them. In an emergency a white frosted bulb will also do, but it should only be a temporary substitute. Particularly for color retouching, *only the blue bulb should be used.*

The slant or angle of the retouching stand is also important. Too straight or too slanted a position makes a great difference in viewing the negative. Figures 5, 6, and 7 offer three views of a retouching stand (and attached retouching device—Fig. 8). Figure 6 shows the proper slant of the stand.

The electric retouching stand is now widely used by large photo studios when volume retouching is done. Retouchers who began working on this electric stand like it and believe it speeds up their work. My personal opinion is that an electric machine is comparable to a fancy car. If the driver of the car is not good, a Cadillac or a Mercedes-Benz will not make him a better driver. The same applies to a retouching machine. If the retoucher does not know how to retouch well, the electric machine will not help him either. This is true of everything else in art. The finest camera will not take a prize-winning picture if the man behind the camera does not know how to handle it; a full box of paints will not create a masterpiece if the painter does not know how to use them. In my years of retouching I have seen beautiful retouching done with a simple retouching desk because of the master retoucher behind the desk. I still believe a beginner should not immediately go to the great expense of acquiring a machine. Once he knows how to retouch, a stationary or electric retouching device will not make much difference to him.

HOME-CONSTRUCTED STAND

Figure 9 shows a sketch of a retouching stand that can be constructed from two simple frames. The frames should be rather thick but without ornamentation, 10″ x 12″ or 11″ x 14″. They can be obtained in any variety store. The upper part should be turned with the frame side down so that the plexiglass can be placed in the groove of the frame. Dowels or four large cork tips can be attached to the second frame to prevent it from slipping around. Two or three hinges will suffice to hold the frames together. Such a stand should be very economical and simple to make, even for a person who does not know how to hammer a nail into a wall. The slides can be of metal or wood, and small grooves can be made on the lower frame for various angle adjustments. For safety a hook can be attached to each side to hold the frames and supports tightly together.

K. WEST RETOUCHING STAND (AND DEVICE)

Anyone who wants to have a professional yet reasonably priced retouching stand will find the K. West patented retouching stand a valuable investment. The advantages of this portable retouching stand are worth mentioning because they cannot be found in any other retouching stand on the market, including the electric machine.

Features of K. West Retouching Device:

1. The device is attached to a folding stand that is no larger than an attaché case. It is sixteen inches long, two inches high, and fourteen inches wide. The complete retouching stand can be stored in a regular desk drawer. When it is opened there is nothing to adjust. Any gooseneck lamp or small table lamp may be used for lighting.

2. The outer ring and adjustable double mask rotate upon a base that rests on springs and will not let you make a heavy stroke.

3. The protective mask is adjustable to any size negative, even to a filmpack size, keeping the negative surface absolutely clean of fingermarks or dust. Thus handling of the negative while working on it is avoided.

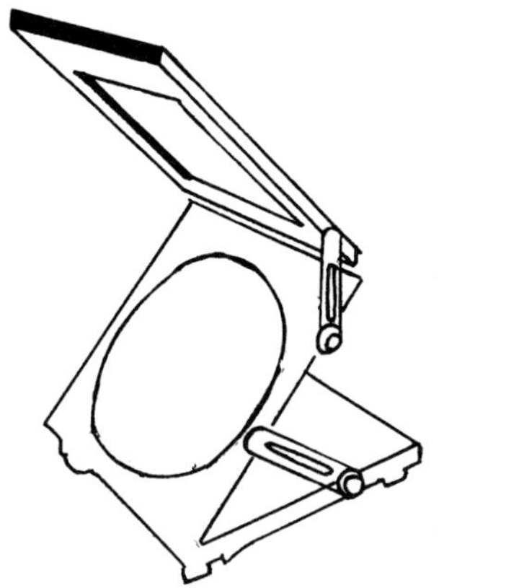

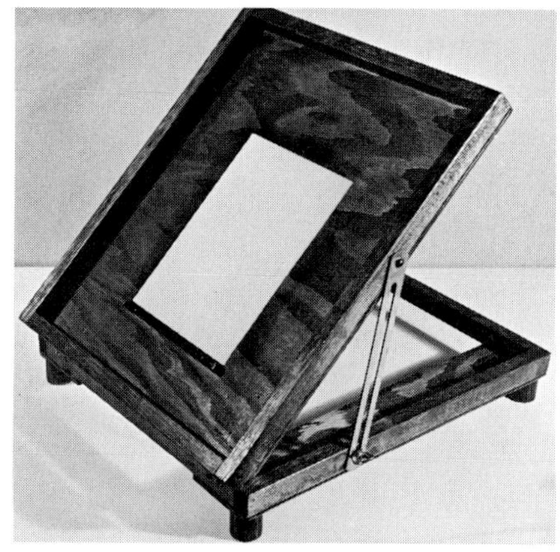

Fig. 9 (Above, left). Outmoded retouching stand. Fig. 10 (Above, right). Home-constructed retouching stand made of simple frames, hinges, and plywood.

The rotation of the retouching surface is unique and important in pencil retouching. The motions of the pencil must move within the skin lines and over facial planes that are circular. Only by turning the negative on the disk can one follow the "grain."

Figure 8 shows the patented retouching device, which can be bought separately and adjusted to a retouching stand or a retouching box already on hand. It is particularly easy to attach to the home-constructed stand (Fig. 10).

Because of difficulty in obtaining retouching utensils in many areas of the U.S.A., all items of the retouching equipment may be obtained by writing to:

NATIONAL RETOUCHERS GUILD
P.O. Box 535
Santa Barbara, Calif. 93102

Retouching Plate

Plates for retouching stands are currently made of plexiglass or lucite. Opal glass was used some years ago but is not much

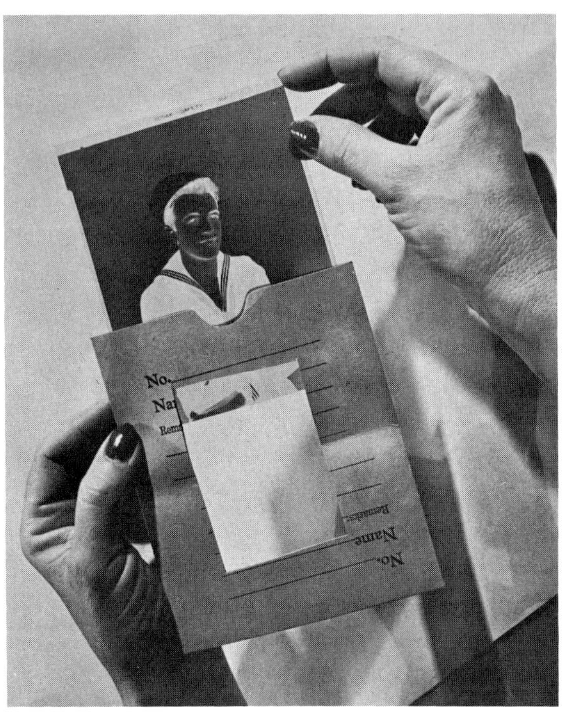

Fig. 11. Negative mask. Unnecessary if retouching stand has built-in mask.

in demand today. However, if you are going to construct your own retouching stand, make sure that there are no flaws in whatever plate you use. A little defect in lucite, opal glass, or plexiglass will show up continually against the negative and will be an annoyance to the retoucher. Always keep the plate clean and wipe it off before sitting down to work. Particularly while the retoucher is etching, the scraped-off emulsion settles on the plate and should be removed. Imbedded specks are best removed with a damp cloth. Then the plate should be gently rubbed dry with a clean rag or cleansing tissue.

At no time should plain ground glass be used for the retouching stand. (Some retouching stands are still equipped with it.) Ground glass is very transparent and shows grain against the light. It may be all right for the viewing box, but it has no place whatsoever on the retouching stand. It strains the eyes terribly and does not show the proper density value of the negative.

Retouching Medium

Before work is done on negatives, retouching medium is applied to give "tooth" to the emulsion surface so it will better accept the graphite. The medium, or "dope" as it is called by retouchers, is a resinous liquid, resembling varnish, that is used on any film or glass surface whether black-and-white or color. The best known makers of medium are Eastman Kodak Co. and Ansco Photo Products. K. West's retouching medium is an especially fine medium. It is easy to apply and leaves a soft, dull finish without ever becoming gummy or sticky.

Mask for Negative

Once the negative is doped for pencil retouching the surface becomes very sensitive to dust specks and finger marks. Always hold the negative at the very corner and put it carefully into the protective mask, if your retouching stand has no protective disk.

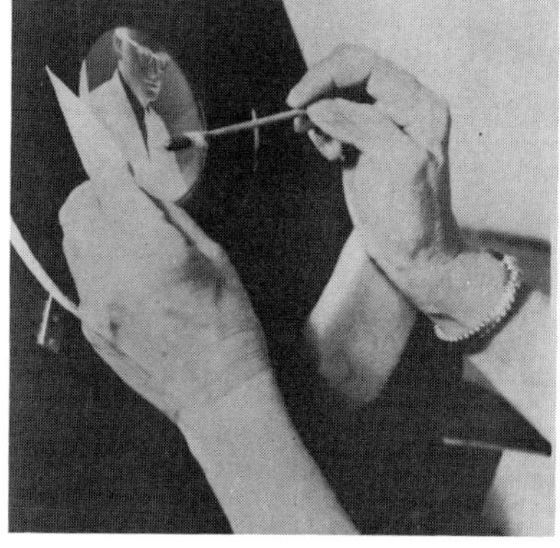

Fig. 12. Holding negative with the corner of an envelope is practical when working with dye, swab, or etching knife. Piece of foam rubber under wrist and especially under elbow increases comfort.

A suitable mask can be made from a brown or black envelope in which negatives are kept. Cut a square or oval-shaped opening in the center to show the head and shoulders of the image. (See Fig. 11.) The mask will not only protect the negative from handling, but will hold back unnecessary light from the background.

NOTE: When working with dye or etching knife, when the negative should be held freely in the hand, cut a corner from any envelope and place it over the lower left-hand corner of the negative (Fig. 12). This is an ideal protection against finger marks.

Retouching Leads

As mentioned earlier, the retouching pencils (more accurately, "leads") match the gradations in negative density. The retoucher needs five or six retouching pencils to match these different negative densities.

5H and 4H are the hardest of the useable group. They will work perfectly on thin and medium-grade densities. Modern photography leans toward rather sharp and thin negative quality. It is always best to start working with an H4 or H5 pencil and then change to a softer pencil.

3H and 2H are next in line for the correction of lines and blemishes on average negatives.

H is the softest of hard leads, and useful for deeper lines and blotches on dense negatives.

HB and 2B are to be used for stubborn lines, pinholes, or removing stray hairs, and are also useful for accentuating a catchlight in the eyes or adding streaks of highlight in the hair. Both pencils are particularly recommended for retouching roll film and color film, where the slick surface of the emulsion will not accept a medium-hard pencil.

Lines and blemishes should be retouched from the start with a softer pencil than 5H, since the density cannot be built up and must be covered with a few accurate strokes. When a hard pencil has failed to remove the line, a soft pencil will not correct the mistake. The line is already filled with graphite and will absorb no more. This particular mistake is usually the beginner's most trying moment. Instead of taking the retouching off and starting anew, the best way is simply to turn the negative to the glossy side, "dope" it (apply retouching medium), and add more retouching to the parts which were not sufficiently filled. It is simpler, however, to use a softer pencil from the start and remove the negative faults with a few deft strokes.

A. W. Faber-Castell and Hardmuth are manufacturers of fine grade retouching leads. A. W. Faber also sells silver leads, which many retouchers like to use because their softness makes them easy to apply to undoped negatives. A short instruction sheet comes with the set.

Lead Holders

When buying lead holders make sure that they are lightweight and finely tapered. Heavy metal holders sold in stores are usually quite heavy, with bulky tips. These are suitable for draftsmen, but cumbersome and tiring for the retoucher. If you cannot obtain a lightweight holder, you will find it available through the National Retouchers Guild.

Abrading Needles

Manufacturers of electric retouching machines supply their special make of etching knives and abrading needles. Demonstrations and explanations as to their manipulation are usually given by instructors or sales representatives. The abrading needle is part of the electric tool with the machine.

Camera stores also have abrading tools for those who do not have an electric machine. The needle is used in many instances to remove pinholes, obstinate blemishes, or stray hairs (showing light against the background) by scratching the gelatine base and thus lightening that particular spot somewhat or altogether. The scratched area will also take pencil without doping the shiny side. However, the point of a regular etching knife also will accomplish the scratching when no abrading tool is available. Detailed technique of this method is explained in Chapter 10, "Retouching Negative Faults." Keep in mind that the abrading needle is not the answer to retouching every line or blemish and should be used carefully.

Sable Brushes

A good retouching brush will be rather short and full, with a point that is flexible but does not drag along. To get the best brush possible spare no expense. The success of dye retouching or spotting depends on a perfect brush, and only the finest No. 000 or 00 sable brush should be used for dye work. One of the best brushes for retouching is made by Winsor and Newton, series 7 (black handle). There are several new brushes on the market, imported from Germany and Switzerland, and Grumbacher also makes good brushes. Carefully select the brush and take your time testing it right in the store. Moisten the tip and see how it keeps the point as you move it over the palm of your hand.

Once you get a good brush, treat it gently. You should not use the same brush for dye retouching and spotting of prints with opaque colors (colors on disks). Also, do not mix brushes when using gray dyes and color dyes.

It is not necessary to wash the brush, but it should be protected with a tip from a drinking straw or put in a special holder. Mishandling a brush by throwing it in a tool box or crushing it into a narrow space of the retouching box will make it useless within a short time. An imperfect point or a dragging hair will make all effort at dye work futile; the good brush can win half the battle of dye retouching.

NOTE: If you have a brush with scraggly hairs do not trim it with a scissors. Instead, dip your brush in water and wipe it over absorbent paper. Then hold it over a burning match for a second or two to singe off the scraggly hairs.

Spotting Colors

These come in liquid or opaque form. The opaque colors are water soluble but are not transparent when applied to the negative. They will cover up pinholes, air bubbles, or other defects which have caused the emulsion to peel off the gelatin base. These colors can be bought in tubes, jars, or on paper disks. They last a long time and can also be used for print spotting.

Liquid concentrated dyes are transparent (as opposed to opaque), and can be diluted by the retoucher as needed for a particular area. Manufacturers of dyes for negative and print spotting have excellent products that have explicit instruction sheets enclosed. They are made by Retouch Methods Co. (Spotone), Eastman Kodak Co., and John G. Marshall Co. (the Webster dyes have been taken over by this company).

Opaque colors are used directly on the negative when a plain white background is desired on the final print, or when objects have to be removed from the negative. In restoration work, photomontage, and commercial photography, the opaquing technique is widely used. Kodak, Craftint, Alvors, Celflex, and Spotone manufacture these dyes. Instruction on their use will be found in Chapter 7, under "Opaquing."

Opaque colors on disks are made by the Talens and Kodak companies, and come in only three colors: white, black, and brown.

Magnifying Glass

The magnifying glass on a gooseneck stand is the most suitable for retouching, if the magnifier is not directly attached to the stand (Fig. 13). It can be arranged to suit the exact size and density of the negative, and can be pushed back and forth easily, which sometimes is not the case with the attached glass.

The size of the glass should be four inches in diameter, no more, no less. It should be carefully inspected for flaws and focus when it is bought. A good one costs about $13.00. Camera

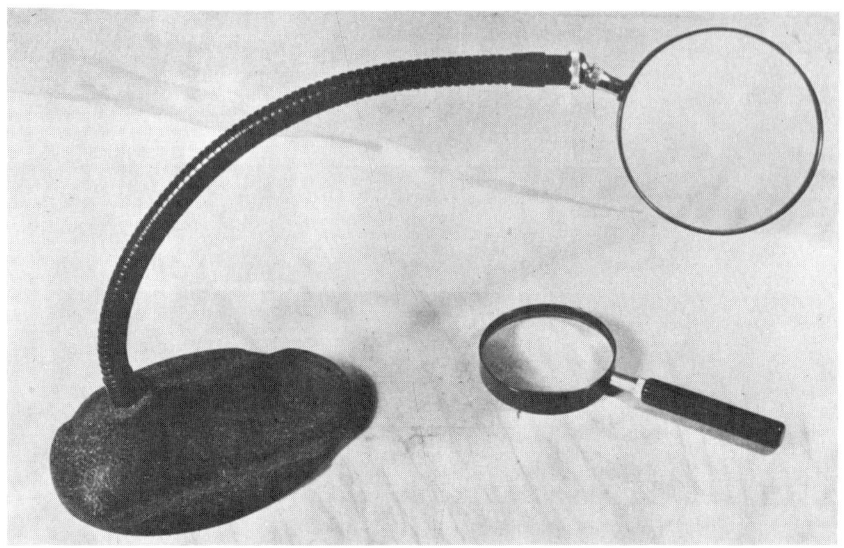

Fig. 13. Magnifying glass on gooseneck. This type is preferable to one with handle, also shown.

stores or pawn shops carry a variety of them. It is advisable to choose from several before deciding which is most suited for one's eyesight.

If your eyesight requires it, by all means use a magnifying glass all the time. However, put it aside frequently in order to view or check densities for overall uniformity. The use of the magnifying glass is always justified when small heads and fine lines and pinholes have to be retouched. It is quite surprising how many flaws one can spot after putting the glass away and looking at the negative from a slight distance.

Never use a pocket-sized magnifying glass or jeweler's goggles. They are a disaster for the eyes. They may be useful for occasional spotting or for a particularly difficult line, but for long and continuous retouching sessions—never.

Another type of magnifying glass has a short holder that is convenient for checking work. However, when it is held for any length of time it causes fatigue. One cannot hold both negative and magnifier comfortably at the same time. With a suitable clamp and screw, this type of holder can be attached alongside or on top of the retouching stand. Make sure it can be adjusted easily and is not too close to the retouching surface. When the holder is too short, the space between the negative and the magnifying glass is too narrow to hold the pencil properly, making a good, direct stroke difficult.

Printing Frame for Proofing

For making sun proofs and observing the stages of progress in retouching, a proofing or printing frame and proof paper are well worth the small investment necessary. Every camera store carries the frames in a variety of sizes, the most suitable being 5″ x 7″. Sometimes one can get a used printing frame. Detailed information on this subject will be found in Chapter 3, under "Making Sun Proofs."

Conclusion

Being a firm believer in the simplest and most efficient way of getting work done, I have, through the years, bypassed complicated retouching methods and unimportant paraphernalia. Having found a product that proves to be most satisfactory for whatever purpose I need it, I stick to it and learn to master it. I often see tool boxes of my students packed with every possible gadget and dye product advertised for photographers. All they do is clutter up the box.

Modern photography has added complexities to retouching. Innovations are a constant challenge, even to the old-timer, who must try them out and evaluate them. Yet learning a dozen methods and never mastering one will not make a better retoucher either. In the end one must decide for himself which method or tool is most efficient in producing satisfactory work.

In order not to confuse the reader with many makes and products on the market, in this book I always mention the best-known supplies, or those I have used. As new products are continually coming into existence in the expanding field of photography, it is up to the reader to choose the products he prefers. My aim in describing certain products is purely to explain *what* to use; the name of the product makes little difference.

NOTE: It is advisable to buy retouching items separately rather than in complete kits in order to get high-grade tools economically.

CHAPTER 3

Preparing for Work

The following steps should be taken in proceeding to actual retouching:

1. Set up retouching desk and adjust light
2. Lay out utensils on right-hand side
3. Apply etching knife or abrasive reducer to negative, if it needs corrections
4. Apply retouching medium on emulsion side of negative
5. Sharpen pencils
6. Insert negative into paper mask and proceed retouching

To insure a comfortable working position, the table on which the stand is placed should be wide enough to hold the utensils and deep enough to allow a margin of five or six inches between the edge of the table and the retouching stand. The table should be high enough so that the worker will not have to crouch or lean over. A bridge table should never be used for retouching. It is neither high enough nor sturdy enough.

The retoucher's elbows should rest comfortably on the table. To be comfortable and avoid sore elbows and wrist, place a piece of thin foam rubber or sponge under the elbows and on the handrest where the wrist is supported.

The chair should be placed so that the body is upright and relaxed. An office chair with a slightly concave back is ideal for the retoucher.

The negative should be placed on the retouching surface just slightly below eye-level. Adjust the light for optimum viewing of a particular negative density; experiment a little to see at what distance light shows defects clearly but does not glare through. Always lay out all the utensils you are going to use. It is unwise to get up too frequently while working, as the eyes get the proper focus after five or ten minutes. Getting up too often slows down the whole procedure of retouching considerably.

Preparing Negative for Pencil Retouching

To ensure a perfect base for pencil retouching, the following steps should be carried out:

1. Put a clean piece of paper or smooth cardboard on the table. Lay the negative down with the dull side (emulsion side) toward you. Have the retouching medium (dope), swab, and cleansing tissues at hand.

2. Dip the swab (Fig. 14 illustrates the correct way to make a swab by wrapping a little absorbent cotton over an orange stick) into the medium. Then press it against the inside neck of the bottle to avoid an oversoaked tip. Holding down the

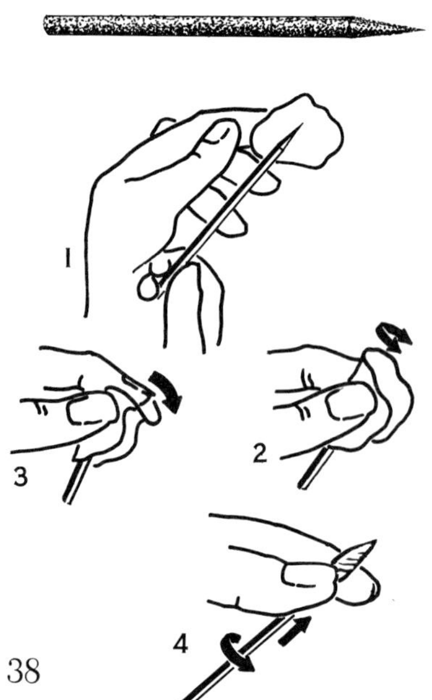

Fig. 14. Art of wrapping skewer for work on negatives and prints. Skewer (or orange stick) should have sharpened point. for detail work. Small piece of cotton is sufficient, with slightly more cotton for larger areas. Procedure: (1) hold skewer firmly against index finger; (2) while pushing cotton over side with thumb, slide cotton over tip with index finger as (3) right hand twirls skewer between thumb and index finger of left hand; (4) make sure tip does not feel sharp. Do not make skewer bulky on sides. Tip must be covered, not sides.

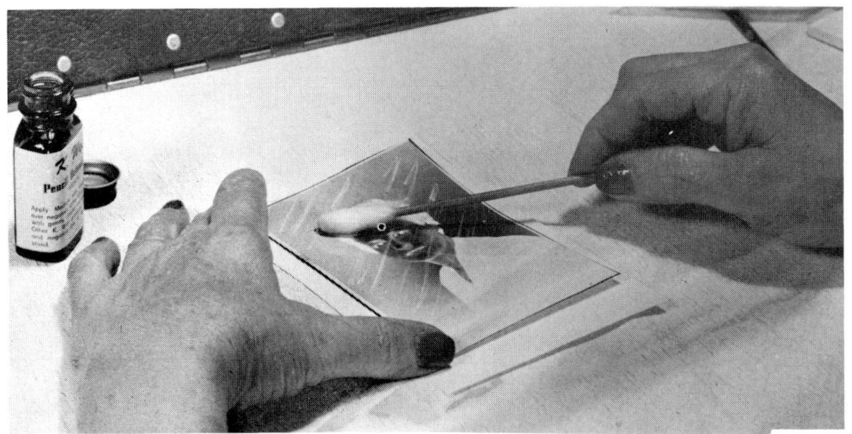

Fig. 15. Applying retouching medium in diagonal strokes over entire negative with swab.

negative with the left thumb and forefinger, apply the medium with several slanted strokes. Move from the upper left to the lower right-hand corner. About six strokes are sufficient to cover the negative (Fig. 15).

Lay the swab aside, at the corner of the table or on top of some object, where the tip will not touch anything. If you put it down carelessly the medium will pick up some speck, and with your next application the negative can be badly scratched by the imbedded dust grain.

3. Quickly take some cleansing tissue, slightly bunched up, and move it gently in large rotary motions over the entire negative, starting at the center, then moving outward and around the rim with a little heavier pressure (see Fig. 16). While applying and rubbing the medium down, *always* bend down and look obliquely against the light to see that the medium is evenly smoothed and has a dull finish. *Never rub hard* or the negative will be polished, and instead of getting a "tooth" the surface will be slick and hard to work on. Eight or nine circular strokes should be sufficient to obtain such a fine finish that a doped area cannot even be detected.

Because most often the success or failure of good retouching

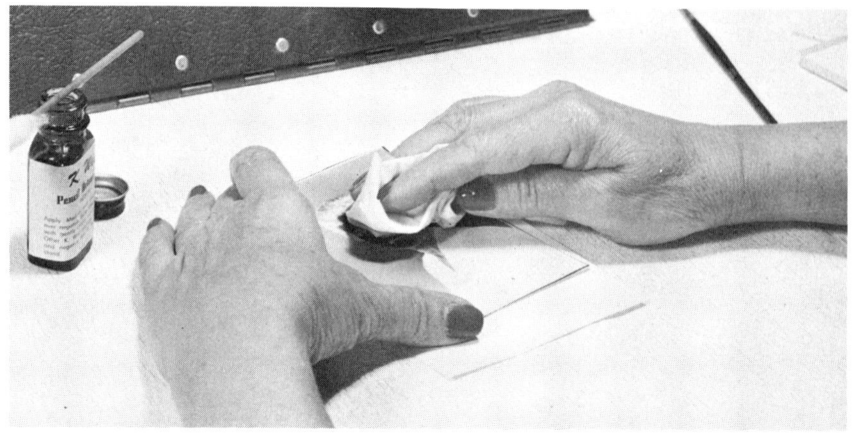

Fig. 16. Rubbing down medium. Gently move slightly bunched-up facial tissue in large circles from center of negative to edge. Six or seven times are enough to give negative dull, even finish. Always work against light to see if rings or hard edges appear.

depends upon how the negative is prepared, these three steps are of utmost importance, and should be followed faithfully. Although some film surfaces have special emulsions that take pencil very nicely without doping, for heavier retouching doping is recommended. Doping is necessary on all film emulsions, whether black-and-white or color.

WHAT NOT TO DO

Never apply medium while the negative is on top of the negative carrier or behind the mask on the retouching stand. You will not be able to see faults of uneven application. Not only will it create a sloppy area on the negative; the glass is sure to get sticky. Do not use absorbent cotton for rubbing down. It is an old-fashioned and messy way and has no place in proper retouching. Many retouchers or photographers believe that by applying only a drop of medium in the center of the negative they avoid finger marks. This point I strongly dispute.

The disadvantage of one-drop application on the negative is that during printing a ring or halo can show up around the head being retouched; a condenser-type enlarger refracts this area. This type of application can cause further difficulty: one might have to correct a fold, or other portions of clothing where the doping did not reach, and would therefore have to add another drop of medium, making this absolutely simple procedure a complex task. The retoucher's first requisite is absolute neatness. If he or she is messy and cannot keep the working table or tools in proper condition, then it is better to leave retouching alone.

Abrasive Reducer

For toning down larger areas of density, such as on a background or highlights on clothes or hair, the abrasive reducer paste (Kodak, about $1) can also be used. *Any reduction should be done before the retouching medium is applied.* Abrasive reducer will also smooth down etched areas on emulsion and eliminate refraction in printing. Since the abrasive reducer is only used in black-and-white negative work, a retoucher may get by without ever having to use it.

TECHNIQUE

Wrap a small wad of absorbent cotton over an orange stick, skewer, or swab; pick up a small amount of the paste from the jar; and rub it over the area with rather heavy circular motions. Keep rubbing till the density shows signs of decreasing. Be sure that the point of the skewer is well covered, as there is always danger the point will penetrate and damage the film. Also, a small piece of soft cotton, a rag, or a scrap of chamois work very well. The procedure is rather slow, but some experimentation on discarded negatives will show how to obtain satisfactory results. An area should not be rubbed too long; rather, overlap edges several times into the surrounding area. Again, sun-proofing will indicate how well the density has been reduced. I would not recommend etching or abrasive reduction directly on the face in order to reduce strong highlights. A simpler technique of minimizing them will be explained in the chapter on Portrait Retouching.

Chemical reduction or intensifying of negatives is most often done in the darkroom, so the retoucher need not worry too much about this phase of retouching. The photographer is acquainted with these methods and knows the chemicals to use.

Sharpening Pencils

Use an envelope or make one by taping the paper together to envelope size, about 4″ x 5″. Fold in half a piece of extra-fine No. 000 sandpaper or emery cloth and insert it into the envelope. Variety stores or hardware stores carry sandpaper of different grades cut in small packets. One can use a rougher sandpaper to start sharpening new graphite and then keep molding it down to a fine point with the finest grade of sandpaper or emery cloth. The type of sandpaper on small boards, sold by art supply stores, should be avoided.

The pencil must be *plunged into the envelope* between two sides of sandpaper to get a sharp point. A piece of cardboard (not corrugated) the size of the envelope will support the pressure of the fingers and avoid breakage of the pencil point. Extend the graphite about one-and-one-half inches out of the lead-holder, insert it into the envelope, and as you move it up and down, keep rotating it.

Sharpening leads is an endless and repetitious chore for the retoucher, but the success or failure of the retouching stroke depends largely upon this particular phase of the job. One cannot stress enough the importance of proper manipulation of the leads. Once pencils have fine points it will not be necessary to resharpen them often. If a point dulls quickly it is a sign of heavy pencil strokes.

I have never found the electric sharpening machine of advantage to the retoucher. The machine has a tendency to make extremely sharp points, in fact so sharp that the point etches into the negative emulsion instead of covering the surface with graphite. For some strange reason, in printing with a condenser enlarger these retouching strokes refract and show up as light cracks on the print.

After having sharpened the pencil, replace the refill to about an inch length into the holder. The retouching pencil should be held lightly but firmly, almost at a right angle, like a dart aiming into the fine lines. (Refer to Figure 6.)

NOTE: Sandpaper need not be changed frequently. With repeated use it becomes so fine that it will not wear down the graphite rapidly and will make a fine point much faster. Figure 18 shows how to hold envelope and pencil for correct sharpening.

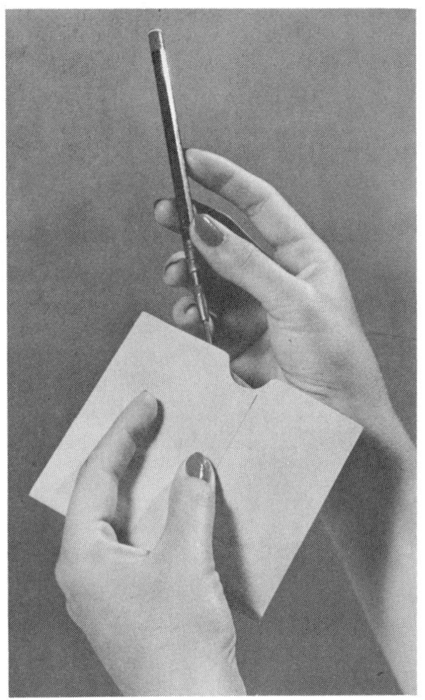

Fig. 17. Sharpening pencil. Pencil should be lightly moved up and down and simultaneously rotated inside envelope. When resharpening, always extend refill from pencil holder to get fine, tapered point. Then re-adjust in holder.

Making Sun Proofs

A retoucher can make his own proof to see the result of his work within minutes. Particularly for the beginner, every practice negative should be proofed to determine progress.

For this purpose one should buy Studio Proof F Kodak Paper in a camera supply store. It is sold in 5″ x 7″ or 8″ x 10″ sheets. A smaller package is more practical, because the paper fades slightly once the envelope is opened. The proof paper should always remain in its original wrapping and be kept in a drawer.

It is economical to cut strips just large enough to cover a head and shoulder shown on the negative.

With the proofing paper one must purchase a printing frame of the type photographers use. The 5″ x 7″ frame is preferable to the larger size, because one usually makes one or two proofs at a time. Two regular negatives can be proofed at the same time, provided they have a similar density. Otherwise one of them will print too dark and the other too light. Holding a hand over the thinner negative sometimes helps to balance the exposure of the negative needing more light.

PROCEDURE

Open the printing frame by pressing down the two springs and turning them out of their grooves. You will notice that one part of the cover is shorter than the other. The shorter part of the frame is used for inspection and helps avoid misplacing the negative in proofing. Put the negative with the *glossy side against the glass of the frame, dull side toward you.* (See Figs. 18, 19.) Quickly cut out a piece of proofing paper large enough to cover the image. Lay the *glossy side* of the proof paper

Fig. 18 (Below, left). Making sun-proof. Place negative against glass with dull side up, glossy side of proof paper down. Then close frame. Fig. 19 (Below, right). Inspect proof by opening one side of frame lid.

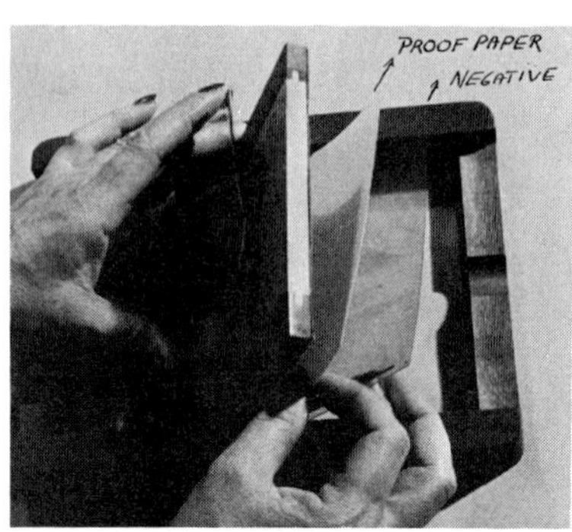

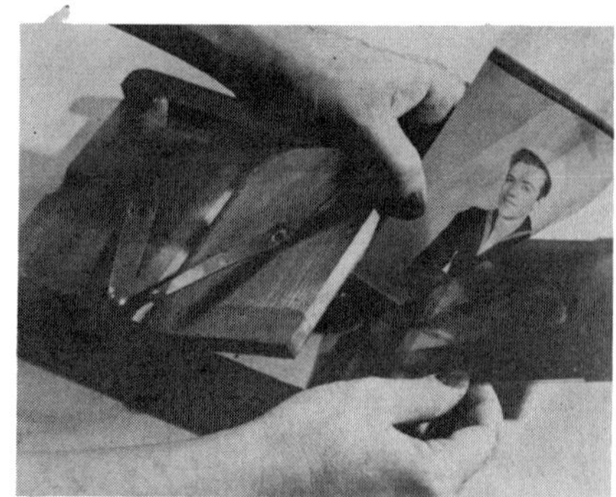

against the *matte side* (emulsion side) of the negative and close the frame, snapping the springs back into the grooves.

Go outdoors and put the frame against the wall or hold it up to the sun for a while. Watch how the white paper under the negative turns pink and then a deeper red, until it becomes quite dark. In bright sunlight two or three minutes are enough for a sharp proof. Dense negatives need a minute or so longer.

To see how far the proof has printed, inspect it. Release the spring at the shorter end of the frame and lift the corner of the proof paper to see whether the picture is dark enough to show detail of lines, blemishes, etc. After a quick inspection, always turning away from direct light or taking the frame indoors, close the frame and leave it in the sun for another minute. The proofs should not be examined too long in daylight and should also be kept away from the strong electric light of the retouching stand. Turn them face down when working on the particular negative. They can be kept in a box or black envelope without losing clearness. This is the way most studios keep them on file.

Sun proofs can be made outdoors even on cloudy days. The brightness of daylight will make a very good proof in five to ten minutes. Many studios do not rely on daylight any more and have special lamps for making "pink proofs." However, the retoucher who does not have this equipment can in an emergency make a pink proof, or sun proof, by placing a 200-watt bulb in the table lamp and exposing the paper and negative to the light till he gets a good proof.

One fact should be remembered, though: the proof is the contact or actual size of the negative image, which means that an enlargement will not look as smooth. Watch for white specks or minute marbled lines indicating uneven or rough retouching. Compare areas on the proof with areas on the negative and work over the parts that need additional blending or other correction. It is particularly advisable to make a proof when etching has been done on the negative, to assure perfect matching of densities.

CHAPTER 4

Pencil Retouching

Pencil Retouching Strokes

In this section I shall present the primary technique of the retouching stroke. Later on, the reader will be given the advanced techniques for finished retouching; even the beginner will have no difficulty following the practice exercises. It will be almost as though he had an instructor at his side; retouching directly on the negatives, he will be able to read and follow the instructions in such a way that he will gain actual experience.

You can judge print quality better if you work on the samples in daylight. Choose a comfortable chair. With a finely sharpened pencil, commence retouching on the negative illustrations. Pencil marks will be slightly visible when viewed sideways on the paper. The same is true of negatives, where the pencil stroke is not easily seen when the negative is viewed over the retouching desk.

An experienced retoucher can determine if too much retouching has been done on the negative, if strokes are long, short, delicate, or rough. In other words, retouching is like handwriting: one can read the negative. No two retouchers have the same stroke, as no two people have the same handwriting, yet the "spelling" in either case must be correct.

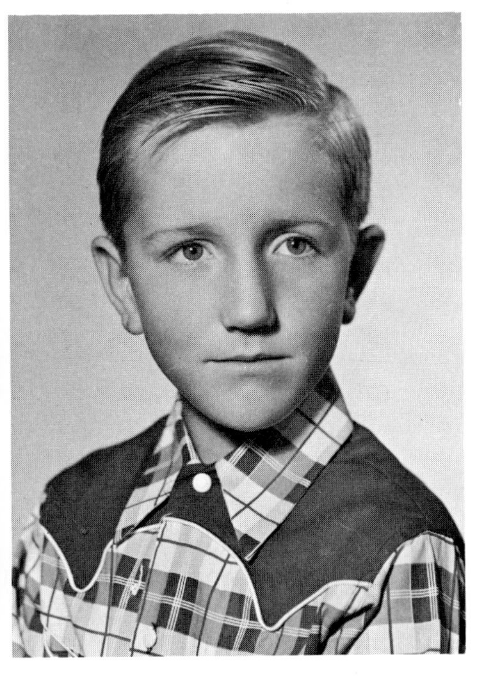

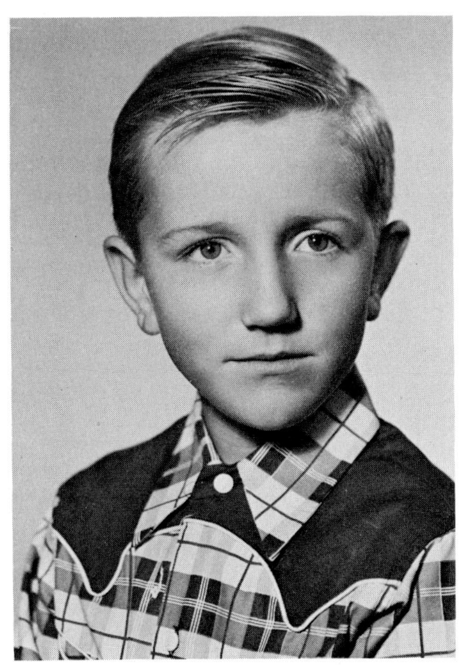

Figs. 20 and 21. Identical negative retouched by two retouchers. Fig. 20 (Left). Required about an hour's work. Fig. 21 (Right). Same negative with more corrections (hair etching, lightening ear on right side) took less than half the time.

Fig. 22. Sketch of basic retouching strokes, greatly enlarged to demonstrate pencil stroke.

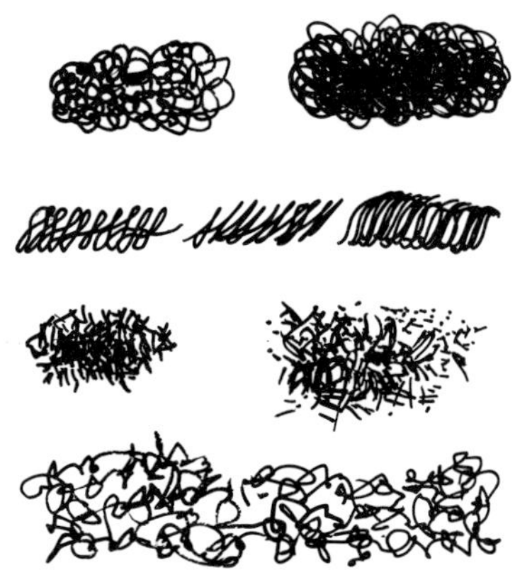

overlapping, filling to surrounding density

the line stroke, scalloped ℓ or S

the poking stroke, commas, dots, dabs

the final blending stroke, "spider-web"

As an example, Figs. 20 and 21 show the same negative as retouched by two retouchers. One covered the entire face with fine pencil strokes, which required about an hour's work. The other retoucher applied only about a fifth of the retouching strokes and achieved in less than 20 minutes the same, if not an improved, portrait. The point I want to make is this: it is *not the number* of pencil strokes that is important in good retouching, but rather *how* and *where* each stroke is placed.

What usually confuses and slows the progress of a beginner is the visual discernment of facial tone gradation. This learning to see every little thing in the negative takes time. By that I mean a few lessons, at the most a few weeks. If the person learning retouching has some talent and perseverance, this phase soon passes, and from then on the going is easy.

Each of the illustrated parts of the face (Figs. 23–33) has different lines and a different skin texture; retouching requires a variety of strokes to blend these textures and approximate the person's overall skin texture.

Fig. 23 (Below, left). Practice negative for strokes No. 1 and 3. Fig. 24 (Below, right). Positive of upper part of face, unretouched.

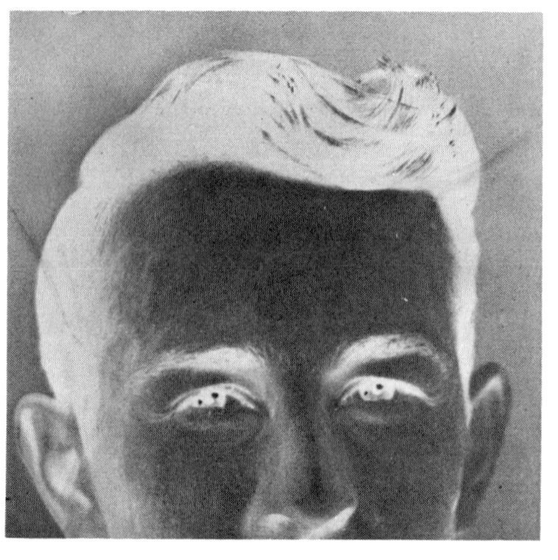

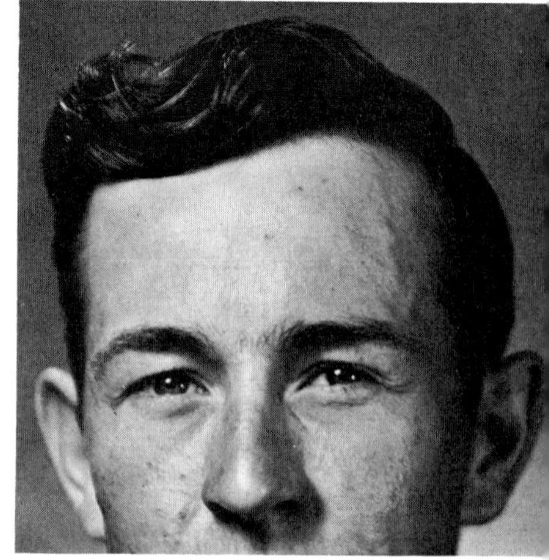

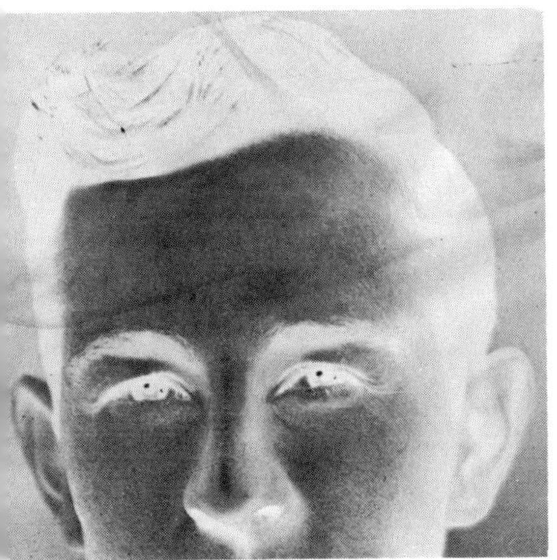

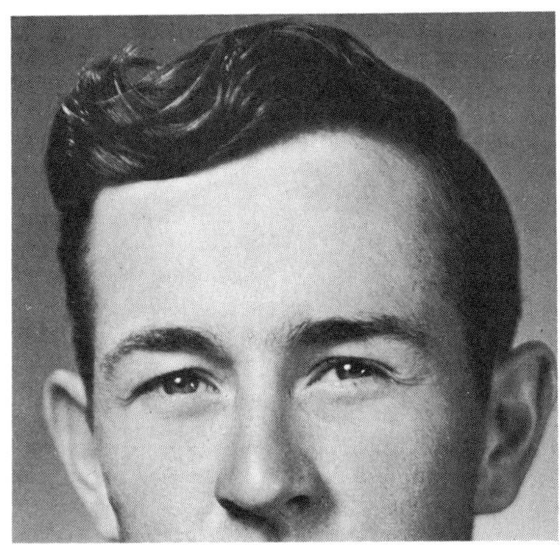

Fig. 25. How partially retouched negative should look.

Fig. 26. Positive of retouched negative. Man's natural rough skin texture was retained, yet harshness of blotches and side shadow were softened.

For convenience in explaining the technique, the basic retouching strokes will be designated by number, as follows:

No. 1. The filling stroke (for adding density): done by overlapping ovals or circles, which one intensifies by repeated application until a desired density is reached. This circular stroke is most effective in retouching the pores of the skin and is used in overall retouching.

No. 2. The line stroke: a finely scalloped or crescent S or 8 motion, which is executed by placing the retouching tool *in* the line (crack) to be retouched, and following exactly the direction of the wrinkle or line.

No. 3. The poking stroke: this will remove blotches, specks, freckles, pimples, moles, and any skin defect. This stroke is similar to doodling or comma motions, dabbing, and cross-hatching.

No. 4. The spiderweb stroke: a combination of all three previous strokes. It is a veiling or pulling-together stroke, weaving its way through various areas, blending, or working around some part needing improvement. This is the final stroke a re-

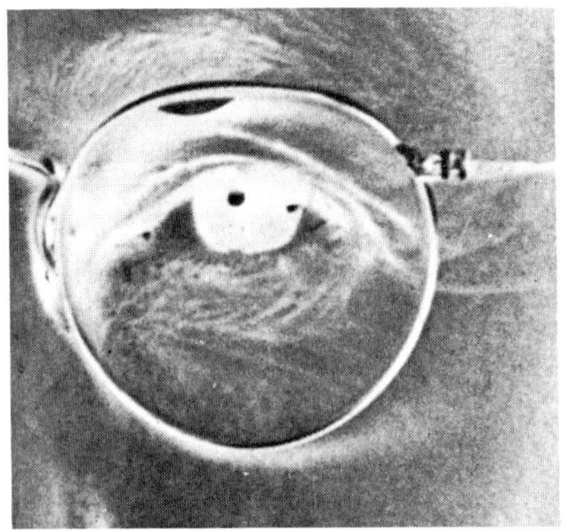

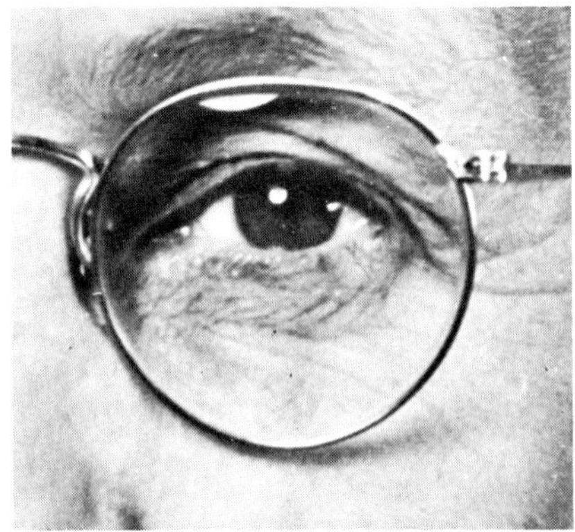

Fig. 27. Practice negative for fine line strokes under eyes. Fig. 28. Observe how each line has its own shape. Pencil stroke must conform to shape of line. (On these practice illustrations the reader can also experiment with K. West Dye.)

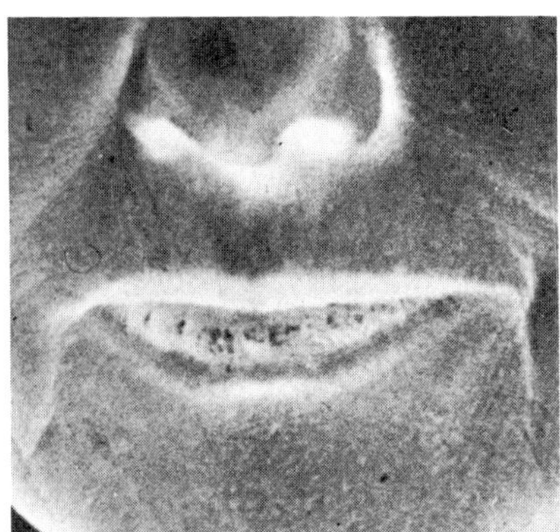

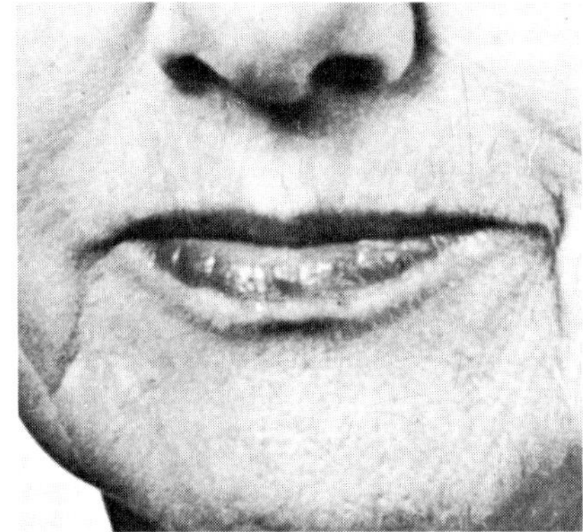

Fig. 29. Most common facial lines on older people. Fig. 30. Lines should be retouched from nostril to mouth and from side of chin toward corners of mouth. Use elongated S or fine scallopped stroke (see Fig. 22).

toucher acquires. This fourth stroke achieves the smooth finish for a print. (See sample strokes, Fig. 22, and refer to Figs. 34-39 for the following text.)

The first practice area is the forehead and area around the eyes, which will mainly require strokes number 2 and number 1.

Insert lead No. 3H or 2H and begin on the left side of the practice sample with a few touches to see if the pencil is right.

Fig. 31. Practice negative for fine poking stroke (No. 3) and blending stroke (No. 4).

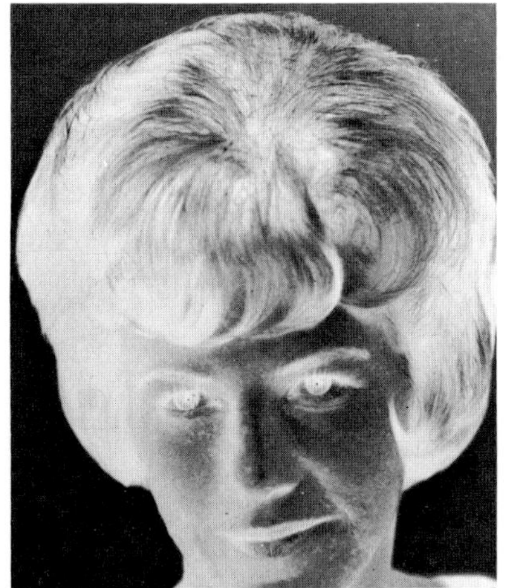

Fig. 32. Positive from unretouched negative.

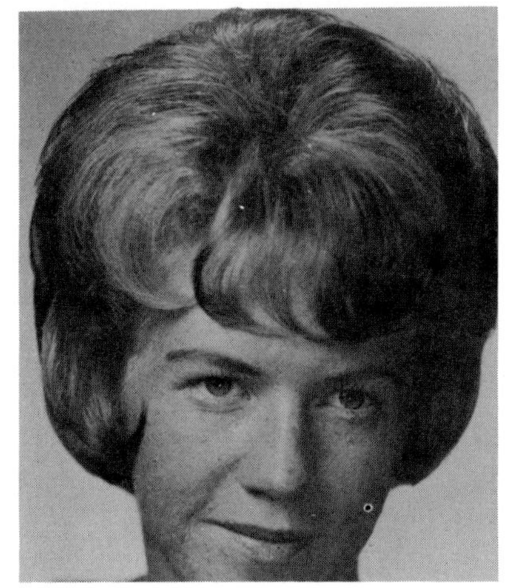

Fig. 33. Print from retouched negative.

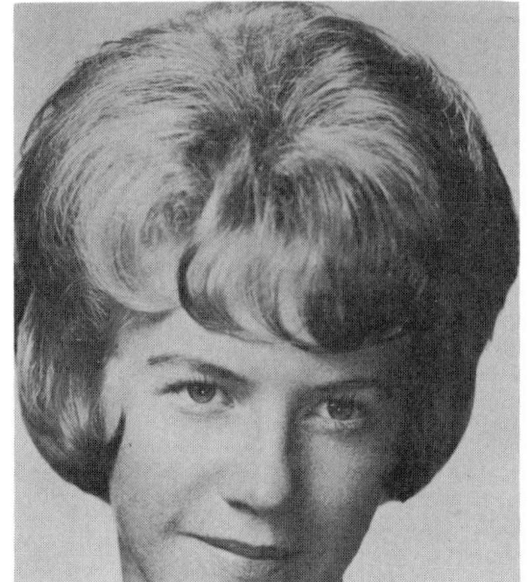

Should the pencil strokes show up darker than the gray tone of paper, change to a harder pencil, 4H or 5H. Bring the pencil in gentle contact with the print. After making several quivering elongated motions with the pencil, you will see the spot or line disappear. You must remember that *the retouching stroke does not resemble a writing stroke or any other stroke you have used in drawing or painting.* It is an absolutely individual touch that every retoucher must acquire.

Try to keep the pencil down when you are doing the line stroke. The hand should be relaxed and the motion should come from the wrist; the fingers should hold the pencil so lightly that if someone pulled it out of your hand you would hardly feel it. If your touch seems too heavy, practice the retouching stroke for a while by holding the holder between thumb and middle finger and keeping the forefinger raised. You might feel an improvement in the touch.

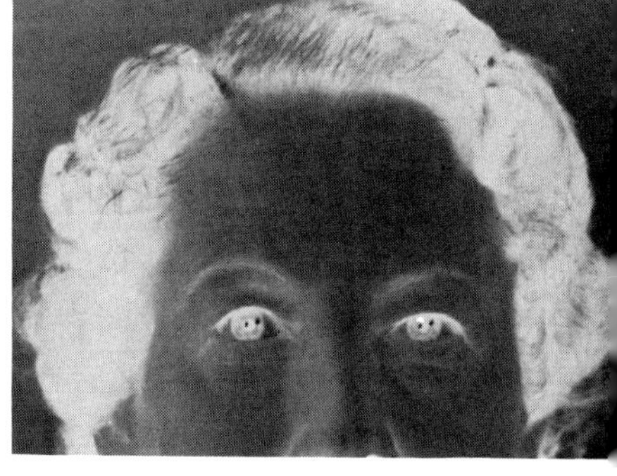

Fig. 34. Practice negative shows mature person's skin texture in need of correction. Use combination of all previous practice strokes.

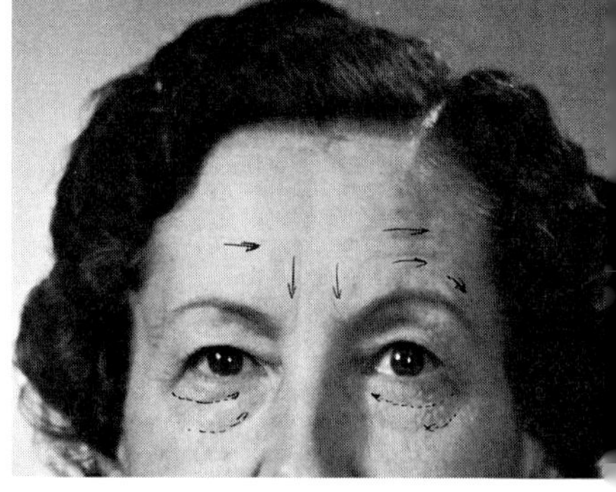

Fig. 35. Print from unretouched negative, indicating direction of retouching strokes.

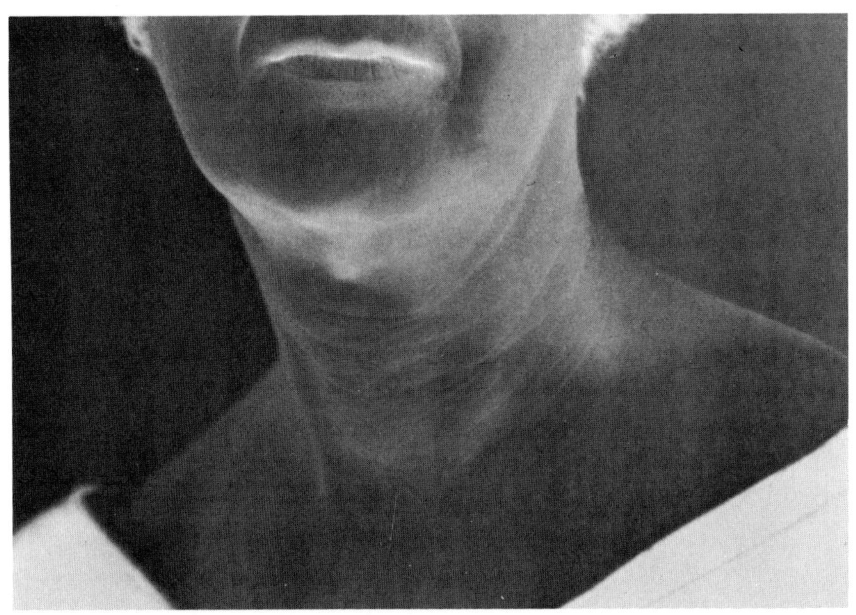

Fig. 36 (Above). Negative of jaw and neck, clearly indicating shape of neck lines. It is important to keep negative rotating in order to keep pencil within lines. Fig. 37 (Below). Print from unretouched negative, indicating direction of retouching strokes.

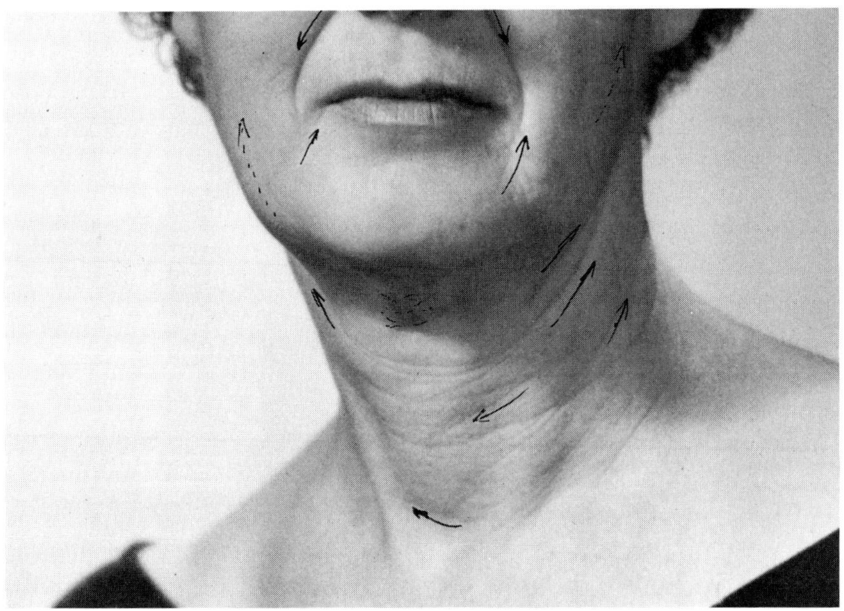

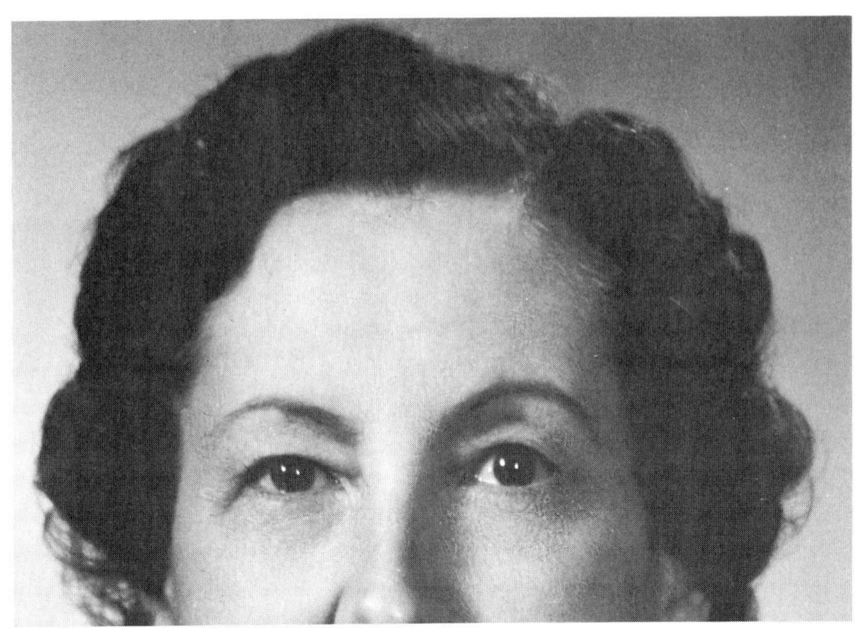

Fig. 38. Retouched print of upper part of face.

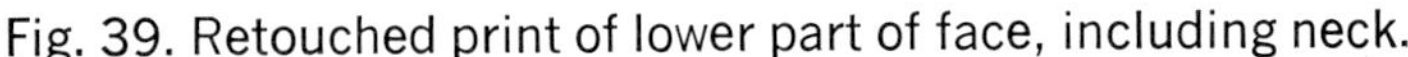

Fig. 39. Retouched print of lower part of face, including neck.

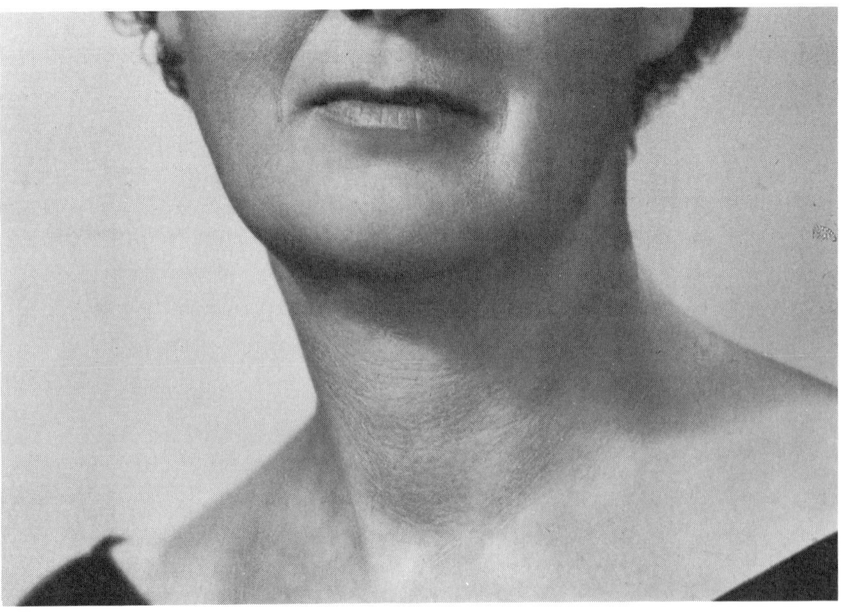

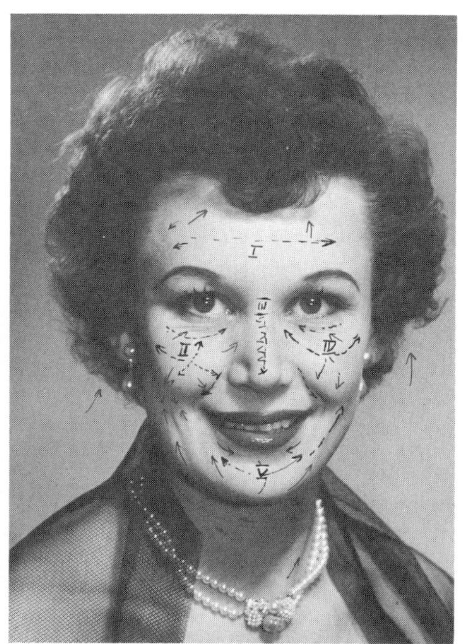

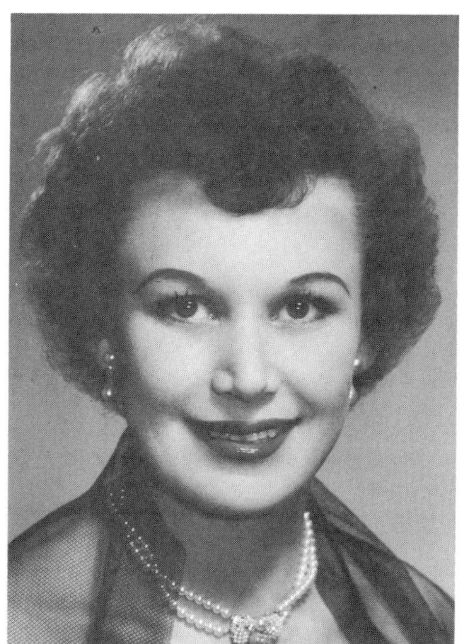

Fig. 40A (Above, left). The five important steps in creative retouching. Lines show way to achieve best retouching results without changing facial expression. Fig. 40B (Above, right). Finished portrait that will please the customer.

Fig. 41A. Not an easy negative to retouch. Strong studio light points up any defect of skin texture. Shadows under eyes and along face were modified by application of dye. For texture correction pencil was used. Eyelids were slightly retouched to smooth sudden change in density from eyeball to side of temple. In such cases retouching eyelids is recommended. Usually photographers use excellent make-up procedures on models for "glamour" pictures, but additional retouching must still be done.

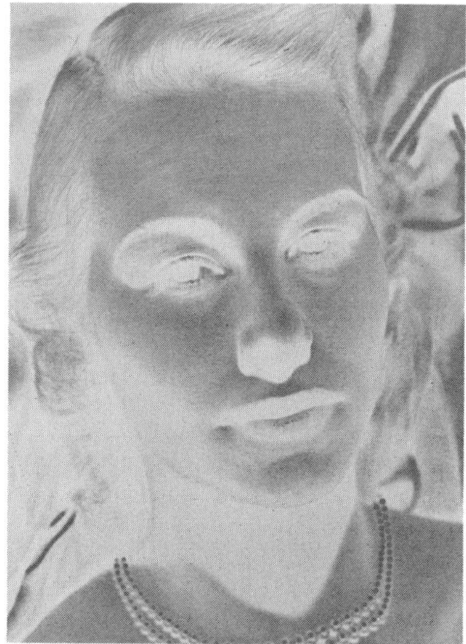

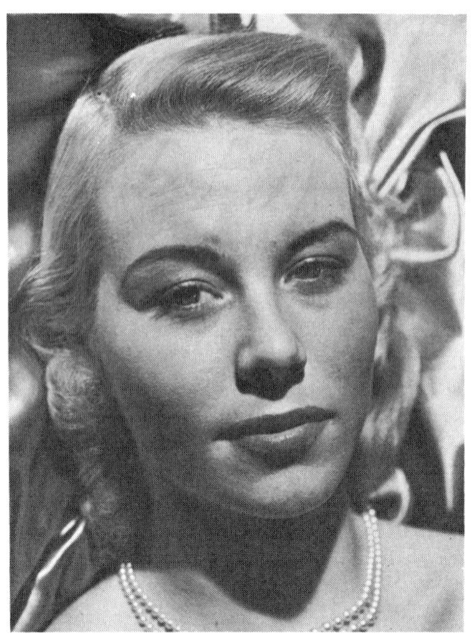

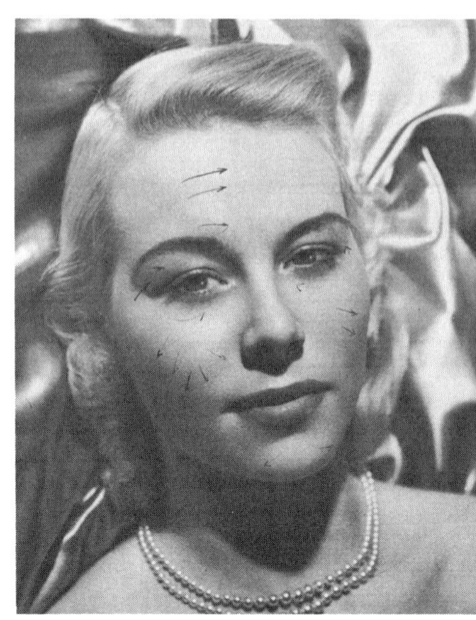

Fig. 41B (Above, left). Print from unretouched negative. Fig. 41C (Above, right). Finished print showing how modeled retouching was achieved. Large head gives retoucher "room to move." Good photographers always supply large heads for such portraiture.

Keep strictly to the light specks and blotches at first; overlapping will show a stronger rim and make the retouching obvious. Keep working across the forehead toward the right side and compare frequently with the retouched sample. After the lines are subdued, one can apply any stroke that would clean up the skin imperfections. How one does it is up to the retoucher. If he cannot see the speck or line on the negative, it will not show up in printing.

The arrows indicating the movement of strokes should be followed. Particularly when working on the neck lines, one should turn the negative sideways to right or left to conform more with the curvature of the neck. (In doing the practice exercises the student may turn the book sideways.)

Systematic Retouching

The retoucher who "wanders" aimlessly about the face on the negative and does not know where to begin, how much to do, or where to finally stop working, is comparable to a traveler without a road map. He keeps going in circles, on sideroads, never reaching his destination on time. So through the years I have developed a systematic process of retouching the face, an unfailing routine that has made first-class retouchers out of the majority of my students in less than ten lessons. If they had not learned it in ten lessons, I advised them to turn to some other vocation.

Figure 40A indicates the five important steps that lead to an unerring good result. They are based on simply following the *natural high points* of the facial structure. These *five steps are all one has to remember* in facial retouching. Regardless of the size or position of a face, it should be retouched in the following sequence:

1. Clean up faults on forehead (either softening deep furrows or cleaning up texture). A left-to-right motion is best.

2. Begin at the outer corner of the left eye near the temple, soften lines under the eye, clean up the cheekbone and cheek in a "sunbeam" motion, to the side of the face (lightly into the shadow, if it is there), then toward the nose and down toward the pockets of the cheek, near the mouth. Continue retouching to the imaginary line that ends below the earlobes and the tip of the nose.

3. Work gently on the highlight of the nose and keep in mind that the nose has a width. It should not appear razor-sharp, which will occur if you run the pencil up and down; rather, give it an effect of roundness by blending along the highlighted area.

4. Now go to the right side of the face, repeating the pencil movement from the right temple or outer corner of the eye toward the bridge of the nose. This way, the natural shape of the hollow of the eye is preserved—always deeper at the inner corner of the eye. It also will not give the bland expression often seen in poor retouching. Duplicate cheek retouching in sunbeam fashion, as on the left side, and proceed downward to the mouth area. Even in a side view of the face, the procedure should follow this pattern. Also clean up the area between the nose and mouth as needed (particularly on portraits of men and older people).

5. Begin on the tip of the chin (where density is strongest), taking in lines that extend down from the corners of the mouth or from the cheeks. Retouch the left jawline first, always moving toward the part around the mouth (step No. 2) where retouching was previously stopped. With a few touches, blend both areas together to form the transition from the upper part of the face into the lower part. Then proceed with necessary corrections from the center of the chin toward the right side of the face with a similar movement.

Retouching on the neck does not follow any particular system; one follows the line movement (as in first practice) and retouches whatever is necessary to make a pleasing effect.

The most important part of this step-by-step procedure, one that seems to be overlooked most, occurs during step No. 5, when one stops retouching on the lower part of the cheek (step No. 2), skips to the center of the chin, and from there moves upward around the mouth and jawline, "lifting" the face, as it were. This does not require tedious retouching, but most often only a few masterful strokes in the right direction. Considering that the cheeks are not as prominent as the tip of the nose or the earlobe, and that they show up in variations of light planes, halftones, and often shadows, it is easy to understand why these motions, which follow the natural grain and bone structure of the face, will preserve or strengthen the character of the portrait *without changing the expression.* Once this step is kept in mind and faithfully followed, the retoucher can master any type of head formation, be it square, oval, young or old.

If we want to camouflage facial faults that appear on the negative, we must follow the methods as discussed above, without wondering how our corrections will turn out. They should and will turn out well, because we have a simple system to follow at all times on all faces, no matter what degree of retouching is necessary.

NOTE: An important rule in retouching is *always to begin retouching strokes from a stronger density into a thinner, or from highlight into shade,* never from shadow toward light, as often is the case in painting techniques. Where the highlighted cheek nears the back of the face the shadow is always strongest, and since photographic paper is not as sensitive as the negative, shadow areas on the face project stronger than they actually are. Softening the rim-shadow on the forehead, cheek, and lower part of face gives dimension to a portrait and compensates for the lack of photo paper sensitivity. (Offset printing of book illustrations, unfortunately, does not do justice to reproductions of portraits and sometimes makes them look flat or too dark. Keep this in mind when scrutinizing the presented samples.)

In the preceding five-step method lies the whole secret of "modeled" retouching, the mastery of the human face as offered to view on the film surface. It remains the only way good retouching can be achieved, and far surpasses any other retouching method, whether it be on black-and-white film, color film, or another substance.

Removing Pencil Retouching

Pencil retouching can be removed by applying retouching medium in the same manner as mentioned before. This will leave the negative clean and ready for more retouching. One word of caution: the negative loses much of its tooth after the first removal of pencil retouching; a softer pencil must be used for the second try. It is best not to remove pencil retouching more than once, as repeated retouching of the same negative becomes futile. More than two applications of pencil retouching should never be necessary. One can apply dope to the *glossy side* and continue covering deep flesh lines on face and neck. Many retouchers do this if enlargements of the picture are going to be made, as it diffuses heavy retouching.

Tips

Do not work fast. The pencil stroking should be done gradually until the desired density appears. If the pencil is moved rapidly from one spot to another, regardless of whether it is being used for a line stroke or any other stroke, lead is applied but no density will be produced. *Stay on* a particular area until it becomes invisible to you or is subdued to the degree you wish it to be. To return to retouched areas is time-consuming, bad technique, and causes *over-retouching*. Resharpen the pencil frequently to keep a uniform, fine stroke.

Now that you have become acquainted with the basic retouching strokes, we shall proceed to advanced retouching, and we shall discuss the entire face, after which you will have a chance to practice retouching.

CHAPTER 5

Portrait Retouching

Part I: Study of the Human Face

No matter what profession a person engages in, his job skills will be enhanced, and he will become more well-rounded, if he learns the theories behind the skills. A good way to study facial texture and muscle structure, and thereby obtain a better understanding of the basis for the preceding step-by-step retouching method, is to examine your own facial contours, in the following manner:

1. Move the fingertips over the forehead from left to right. The fingers will glide smoothly without tension and without pulling the skin. Now try moving the fingertips from the eyebrows up toward the hairline. Observe how the skin bulges and there is a feeling of moving "against the grain."

2. Move the fingertips in a curved motion from the side of the nose over the cheekbone to the earlobe; they glide lightly over the surface of the skin. Again: from the center of the cheekbone (under the eye), draw the fingertips down toward the jawline. Feeling the pulling sensation and seeing the face becoming thinner and older is very, very convincing!

3. Start from the center of your chin and let the fingertips glide along the jawline up toward the earlobes. Do it with both hands and hold the fingers at that point for a while. The jawline will appear firm and youthful, rounding out the lower part of the face into a pleasant expression without lifting the corners of the mouth.

The practice pictures in this chapter will help the reader to acquire the habit of retouching in five steps. Each poses a different retouching problem that is explained in the caption.

Only basic directions can be presented in a book, and the few examples given should be considered purely as a guide in evaluating a negative. Each face requires a "diagnosis" before one begins to retouch. After many years of retouching, I find I still have to study a face and determine what I want to do to improve it.

Observation of the human face as such—forgetting the skin faults for a moment and getting a general impression of facial structure and planes—is something that the retoucher should learn. Wherever you are—on a streetcar, bus, train, or sitting in a crowded room—*observe people!* Without being obvious about it, retouch their faces in your mind. Would you remove that second line under the eyes, would you soften that furrow between the eyes, would you take out the drooping lines from the corners of the mouth? I did it when I started retouching many years ago and do it to this day. Painters do it, writers do it, so why shouldn't a retoucher do it? It would help many a photographer to be more observant of people; it might help him to pose them better. Some knowledge of retouching would also make him more aware of facial lines which are often needlessly exaggerated by bad lighting.

Types of Faces

The retoucher working on a negative is confronted with many problems, not only those connected with skin texture and age; he should therefore be aware of the type of face with which he is dealing. The awareness of the type to which a particular facial structure belongs will enhance his retouching technique in that he will know when to subdue one area and accentuate another.

I propose that there are five facial types (with variations), based on the shape of the face. I have found that by judging the outline, width, and length of the face, from the earlobes to the tip of the chin, one can quite easily determine the shape category of any face. The categories are:

1. The oval face: (Fig. 41)
2. The long face: (Fig. 42)
3. The square face: (Fig. 43)
4. The heartshaped face: (Fig. 44)
5. The round face: (Fig. 45)

The structure of these facial types is quite distinct in young people, and generally the face retains its typical character throughout life.

The illustrations, which represent only the most common facial types, indicate how to effect the various improvements on each type of face.

Even in a character study, discriminating retouching, softening a harsh shadow or a few distracting lines, will improve the study.

Facial Structure in Relation to Age

No two faces are alike, just as no leaf of a tree or flower is exactly like another. We *resemble* each other, having two eyes, a nose and a mouth—but the *structure* of each part is so minutely different that even identical twins can be distinguished by some small difference in features.

At each stage of life the facial formation has particular characteristics. (We shall not talk about body structure, as we are mainly concerned with facial features.) Both the photographer and the retoucher should be intelligently informed about facial structure. Their teamwork can produce a portrait: the cherished record of a human being that begins when the camera shutter clicks.

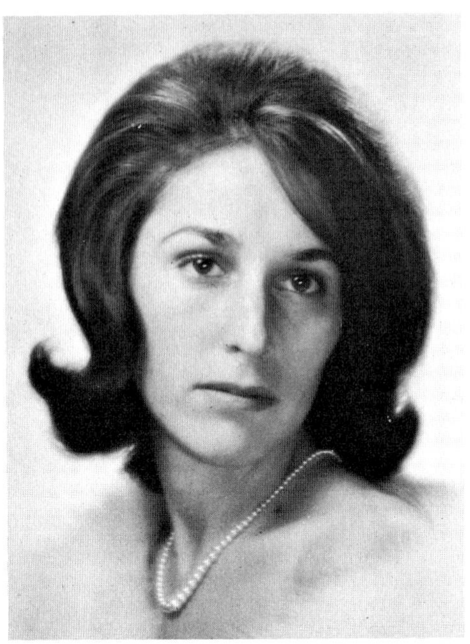

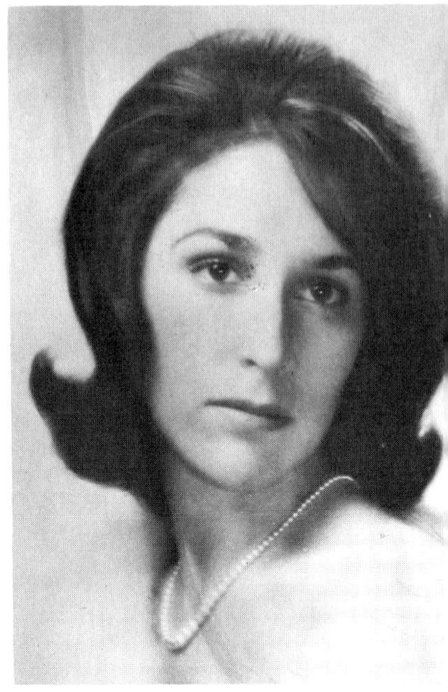

Fig. 42A. Elongated face with protruding cheekbone and uneven hairline. Fig. 42B. Finished print. Etching smoothed down strong cheekbone. Hair was etched on both sides of head. Nose was modeled slightly for better appearance. Streaks from inner corner of eye were removed. Face appears happier.

We will touch only briefly on a few important "Stages of Man" and point out their characteristic appearances:

1. Child: The head is quite large in proportion to the body, face is fleshy, skin texture smooth and firm.

2. Young person: Features are stronger, shape of head is clearly defined. Skin shows individual texture: oily, dry, fine, or coarse.

3. Mature person: Character traits have etched themselves into pronounced expression, showing slight wrinkles, narrowing of cheeks, and bonier or waning jawline.

4. Older person: Cheeks and jawline have lost their firmness, eyes are set deeper, nose seems sharper, and area around mouth has lost its fullness. Skin seems porous and neck has fine wrinkles.

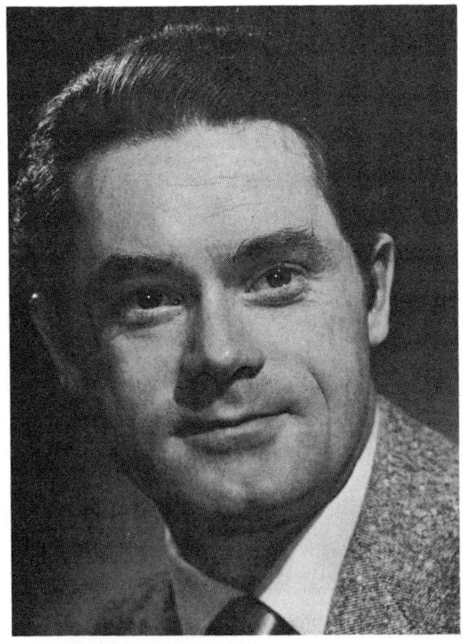

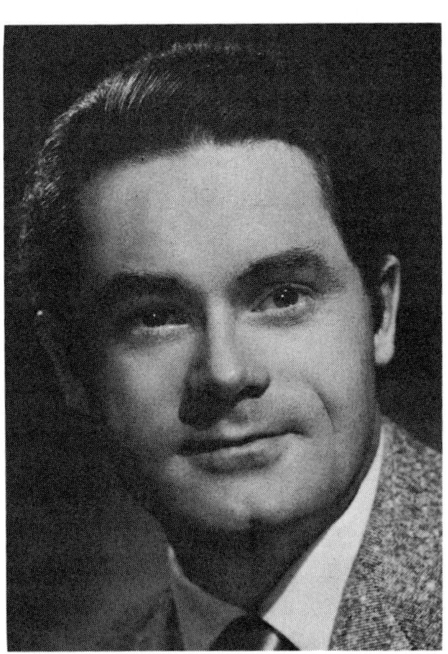

Fig. 43A. Square face. Fig. 43B. To minimize width of face, shadow was preserved as much as possible. By strengthening nose somewhat, cheeks seem to recede. How much retouching should be done on such a face depends on purpose of picture. Entertainers like portraits retouched more than the average person.

Fig. 44A. Heart-shaped face. Although little seems wrong, "glamour retouching" required careful retouching on entire face. Lower part of face always needs retouching. Rather short nose was improved by strengthening highlight on nose. Hair on nape of neck was filled out and neck etched down to make it appear thinner.

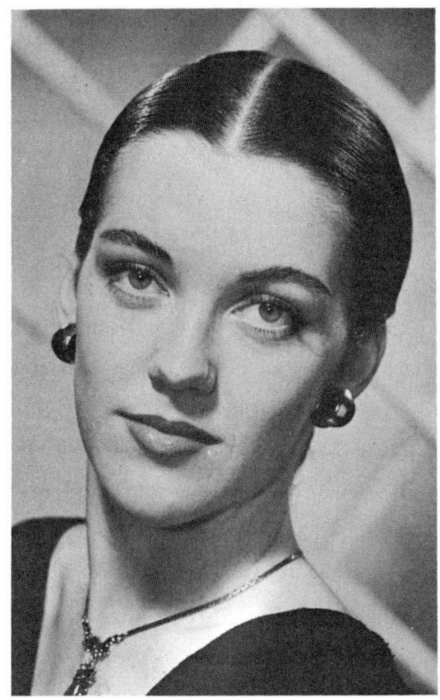

Fig. 44B. Retouched print. Can be used for advertising and publicity purposes.

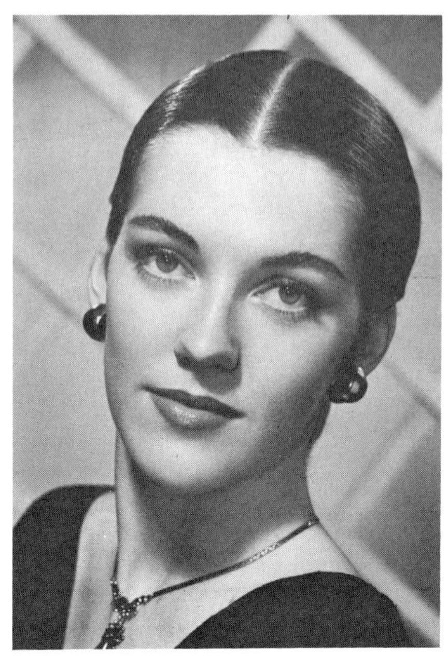

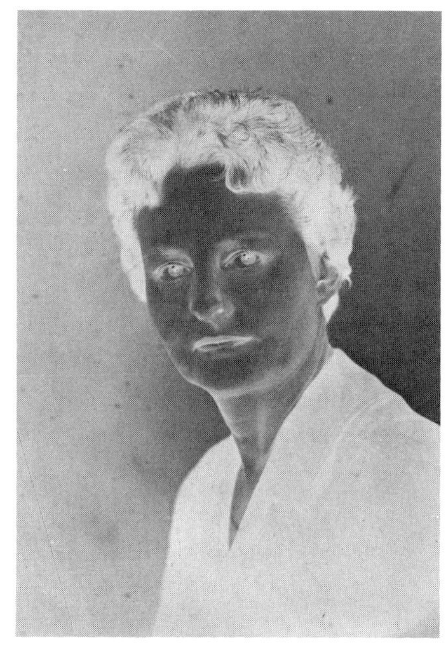

Fig. 45A. Mature person with round face, without glamour pose. Normal-to-dense negative like this is not hard to retouch.

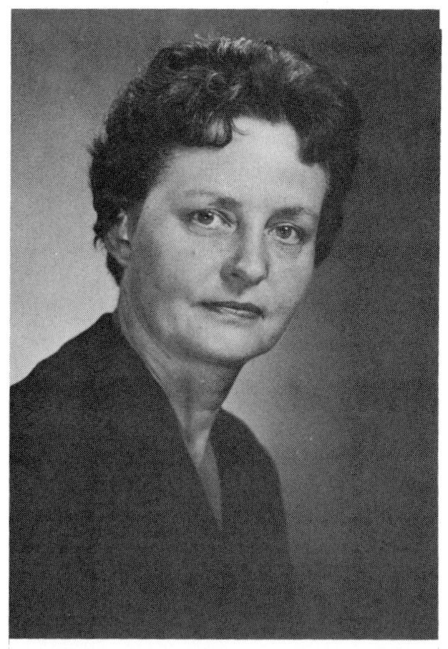
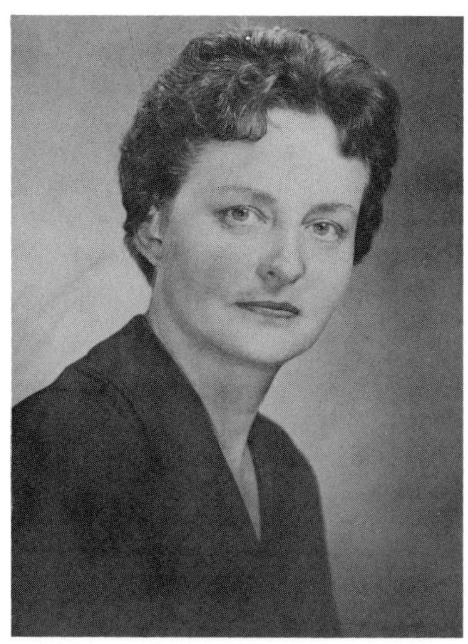

Fig. 45B. Print from unretouched negative. Hairline needs etching; mole, skin texture, jawline, and neck all need improvement. Fig. 45C. Finished print retains pleasant expression of sitter. Avoid etching jawlines unless you are an expert etcher. Simple jawline correction can be achieved by retouching from neck up and removing lines running from side of face down. If necessary, a little print spotting with dye will improve jaw outline. Removing drooping corners of mouth helped expression.

In the following pages, we will discuss each type as briefly described here, and will point out in what way portraits of these types have been improved.

Part II: Portrait Retouching by Age of Subject

Portraits of Children

Considering the lovely features of a child, the petal-soft skin and the sparkling eyes, it is no wonder that the opinion prevails that a child's portrait need not be retouched at all. Still, a few points have to be considered before corrective work on children's pictures is condemned.

For instance, the chubby cheeks of a child form dark circles below the eyes under strong studio lighting. Also, a baby's

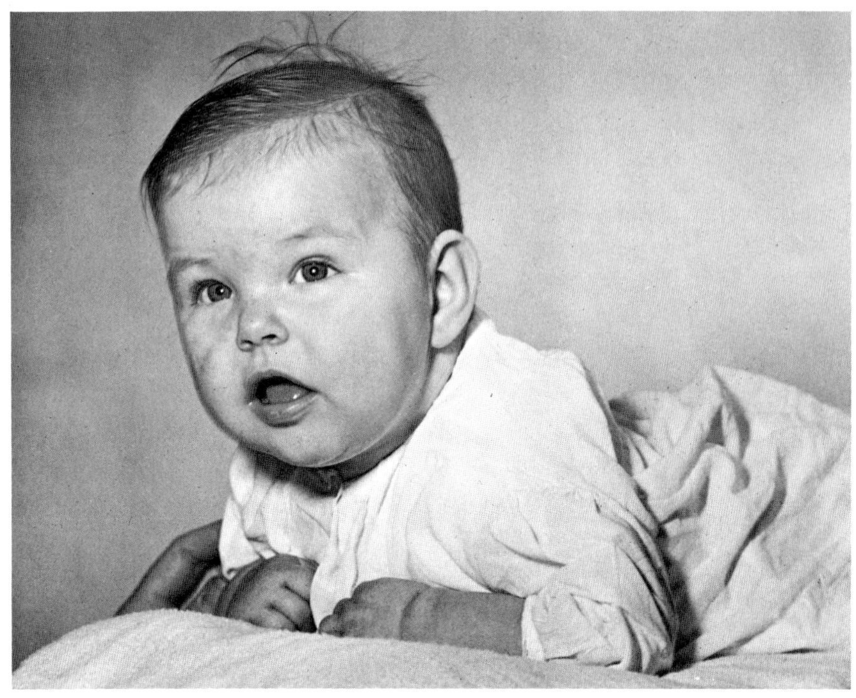

Fig. 46. Even picture of pretty baby needs some retouching. This example will be used again in discussion of opaquing-out backgrounds (see Chapter 7).

cheeks are "puffed up," and when he is smiling they create an overstrong shadow between eyes and cheeks. That cute little double chin that looks so adorable shows up as a deep crease of flesh on a photograph. Unruly hair is distracting and needs the retoucher's help. The etching knife can be used to fill out thin strands of hair, or they can be removed from the background with pencil and dye. (See Fig. 46.)

Freckles are a controversial point of discussion: shall they be left in all their glory, removed, or subdued? It is up to the photographer to abide by the wish of the parents. One thing must, however, not be forgotten: freckles are just a slightly deeper red-brown than the skin tone, but on a black-and-white print, they show up as black spots or blotches that attract undue attention. When freckles are so numerous that they give a smudgy appearance, whether it is on a child or a grown-up, retouching is wholeheartedly recommended. Even a softening of the most obvious freckles and blotches will improve a picture and still retain the impression of freckles. (Refer back to Fig. 33.)

Contrary to general belief, retouching a child's skin is very difficult, even for an experienced retoucher. Photographers do not want to pay much for this type of work because they think that all a negative needs is to have a few lines removed. However, even the few touches have to be done with a delicate touch and know-how, because a child's skin does not have the porous quality of a grown-up's; there is practically no grain to "put the pencil on."

Another handicap for the retoucher in baby portraiture is that sometimes a photographer takes a picture of a whole figure and then decides to print only the head and shoulders, leaving the retoucher a pea-sized head to work on. Only more important defects can be corrected on something this small. Working on the slick side of the negative with a soft pencil helps.

Knowing how to correct a broken or misshapen tooth is essential in children's portraiture. Technique: define the shape of the tooth with a 2B pencil and the point of the etching knife or abrading needle. First fill in with pencil to get the shape (making it white on the print) and then etch a fine line to make the darker separation from the adjoining tooth.

A blurry catchlight in the eyes gives an out-of-focus impression to a photograph. Make a clear-cut highlight (dark spot on negative) with the 2B pencil on the emulsion side. If there are too many catchlights, leave spotting till the print is finished and then match the right tone and effect with appropriate spotting dye. This same technique applies to any portrait.

The discerning eye of the retoucher will probably always find some room for improvement in a child's portrait. Although the volume baby picture studios do not keep a retoucher very busy, there is a great difference between a portrait of a child and an enlarged snapshot of a youngster.

Portraits of Young People

It is most lucrative for the retoucher to cater to photographers of school children, from youngsters to university students.

The main retouching jobs on young people's portraits consist of texture clean-up, shaping highlights, softening lines under eyes, or subduing laugh lines. Often the retoucher would like to suggest to the photographer not to take so many portraits of children laughing, because they involve more corrections than would normally be necessary. Often that supposedly happy expression turns into a stereotyped grimace, distorting the face and not improving the looks. Instead of being a friendly expression with a smile from within, the grin sets in motion about sixty muscles, resulting in a toothy look that says "cheese." Even on a chubby youngster, the laughlines break up into two or

Fig. 47A (Below, left). Negative of this picture is Fig. 2. Positive print shows uneven skin texture and strong empty spaces in hair near neck. Fig. 47B (Below, right). Print from retouched negative. Observe how nose was improved by slight modeling. Shape of lower eyelid was retained, hairline improved on both sides of neck. White space near left shoulder was spotted down with dye on print. One could also have etched in hair.

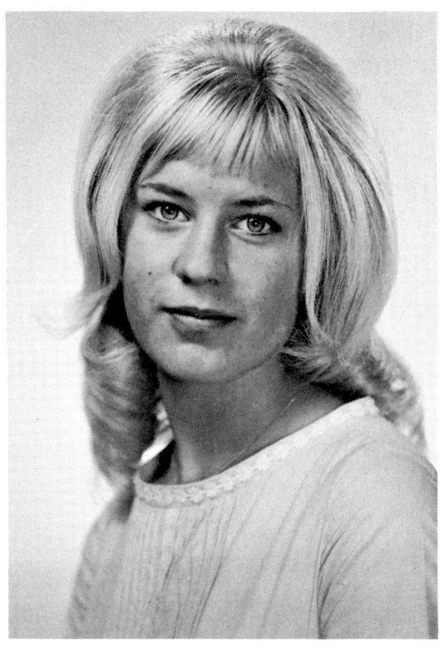

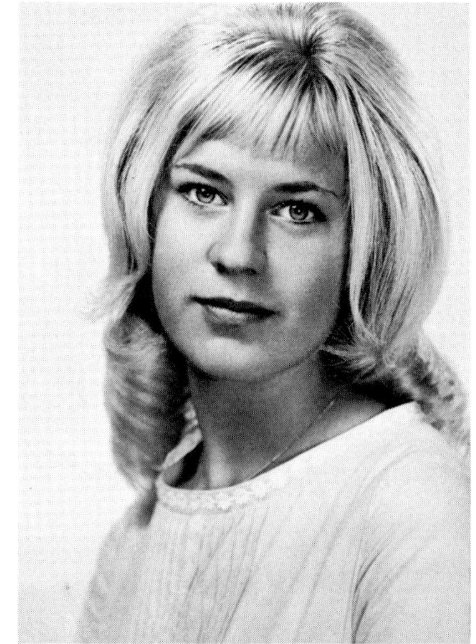

three folds, leading from mouth to chin, distorting the lower part of the face and jawline.

On portraits of older people it becomes an even bigger chore to tone down these faults of posing. Often when I work on such a negative, I can almost hear the photographer say, "How about a nice, big smile?" And I feel like saying, "Please, Mr. Photographer, remember the retoucher!"

The picture of the young girl (Fig. 47) required light texture retouching on both sides of the cheek and filling in a little density toward the side of the nose. The gentle poking stroke (No. 3), and strokes No. 1 and 4 were mainly used. Under the eyes the scalloped or elongated "8" strokes softened the lines but did not distort the shape of the lower eyelid.

School negatives usually require etching hairdos, adding or filling in gaps, fixing straggly bangs, etc. The beginner has the best chance to learn touch and speed on these negatives, because they do not require the demanding "glamour" retouching of the high-priced studios and yet pay as well, if not better, in the long run.

Portraits of Young Men

Although a woman's portrait can stand quite a bit of retouching, to me there is nothing more obnoxious than an over-retouched picture of a man that gives him a doll-like expression with a pancake make-up texture. The retoucher has much leeway in strengthening features, accentuating highlights not sufficiently pronounced, or decreasing those that, because of the bonier structure of a man, may be too pronounced. Bear in mind the purpose for which the portrait was made. Is it a character shot of a masculine, rugged sportsman or worker, a portrait of an intelligent, sensitive executive, or a casual picture of a young man with a smile and mischief in his eyes?

For the "man of distinction" portrait the retoucher must supply a good clean texture. It is mainly the "five-o'clock shadow" that needs to be worked on. Lines under the eyes

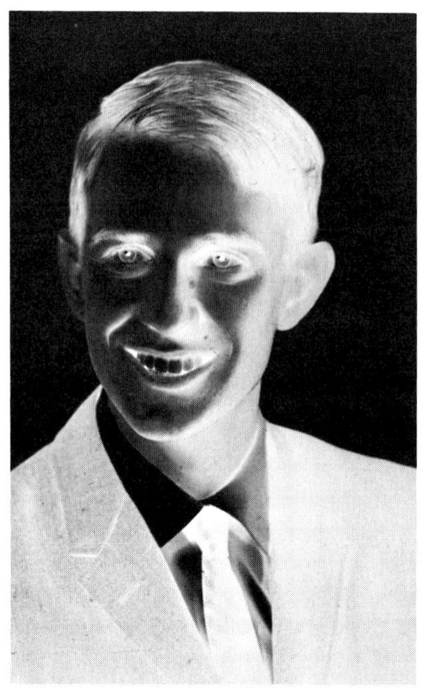

Fig. 48A (Left). Typical school-photograph portrait. Negative indicates strong lines under eyes and mouth. Also, contrast between cheek and side of face is too strong. Fig. 48B (Below, left). Print from unretouched negative. Fig. 48C (Below). Retouched print shows softened lines, light blending along side of face, and corrections on chin. School-photograph retouching is extremely lucrative for retoucher, who can do several in an hour.

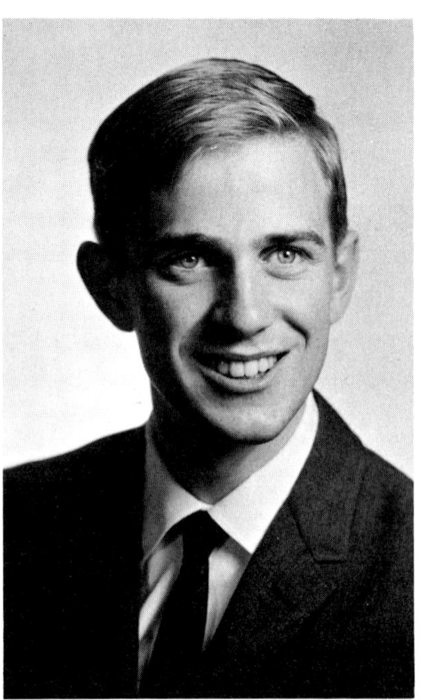

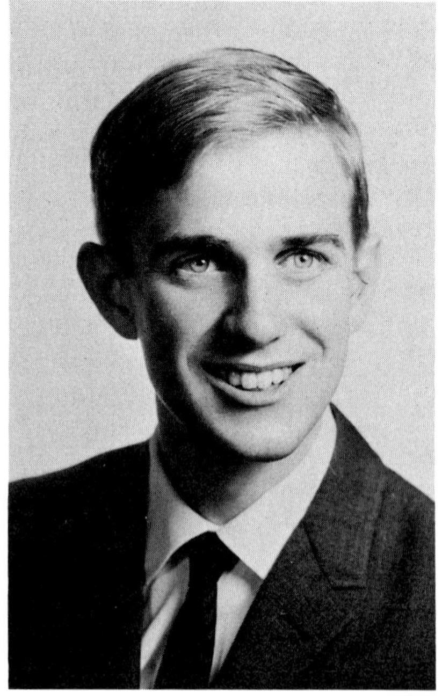

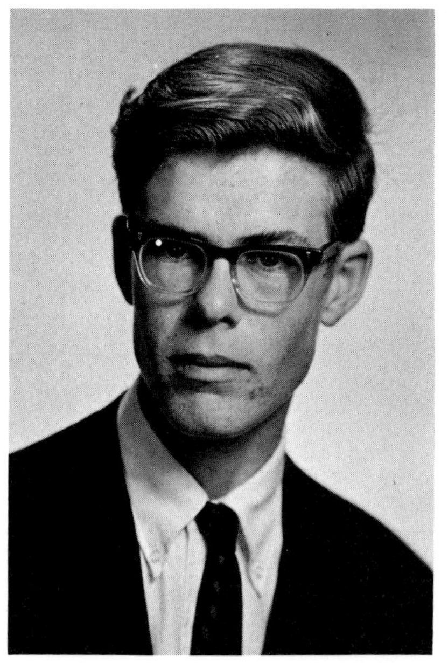
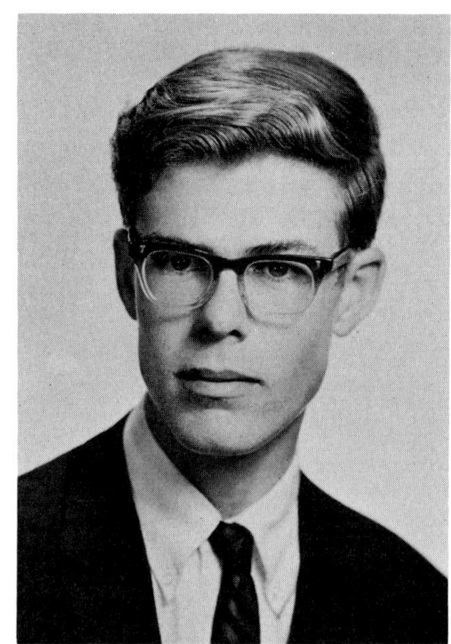

Fig. 49A. Unretouched print. Since many people wear glasses when they are photographed, eyeglass shadows frequently appear in portraits, and must be retouched out. Dye retouching is ideal for removing them.

Fig. 49B. Light pencil retouching was also used. Observe how face appears wider when sunken-in effect under cheeks has been removed. Spot on eyeglasses was etched out with regular etching knife.

should be softened, the nose distinctly formed, shadows subdued along the bone toward the cheek where it slopes abruptly into the face.

Retouching pictures of men in their twenties frequently requires only light complexion-cleaning. A rejuvenation will not be appreciated by these clients. They prefer to look mature rather than as though they had just left school.

When a stray hair or an uneven hairline is present, one can either retouch out the hair against the background or if necessary for better appearance fill it in with the etching knife. Twisted ties and creased shirt collars should be carefully retouched with pencil or etching knife, as the case may be. These rather difficult-sounding corrections are really not complicated once the rudiments of knife and pencil use have been comprehended and mastered.

Figs. 48, 49, and 50 are examples of young men's portraits. Figure 50 is a perfect illustration of a retouching problem we talked about previously: that wide grin. This picture not only presents the problem of subduing the laugh lines, but also the problem of cleaning up the skin texture. Also, the shadow along the side of the face needs a softer transistion to the back of the face. Because of strong studio lights in black-and-white photography, which lacks the shade of color of the natural skin tone, this particular area always requires some retouching in order to give dimension and good tone to the print.

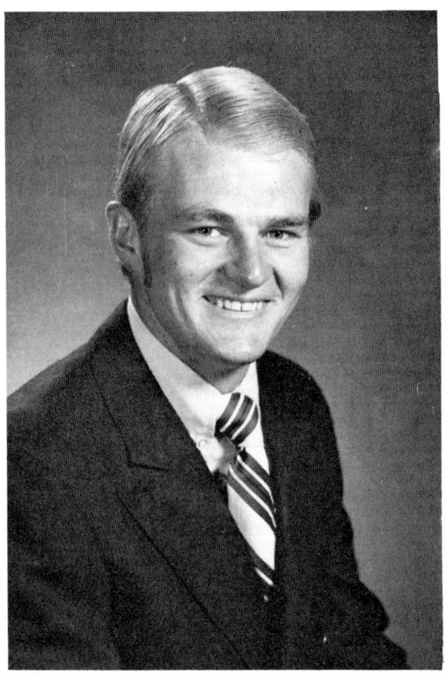

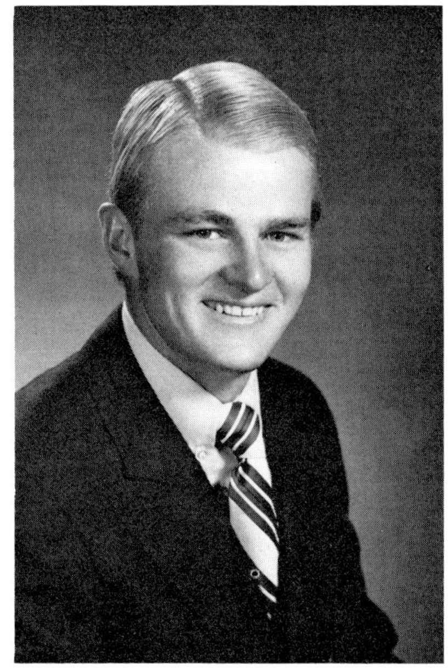

Fig. 50A (Left). Print from unretouched negative. This type of negative is hard to retouch. Retoucher must not only subdue strong shadow areas, but must correct texture and too strong laugh lines. Fig. 50B (Right). Stray hair was spotted out on print for easier matching. Retouched negatives always print up a little lighter, because dye and pencil retouching give more "body" to film surface under enlarger.

The balancing and light blending of one density into another is what is called "modeling" in retouching terms. Following the systematic method of retouching previously explained, by taking care of one part of the face after another, the retoucher will develop the speed for overall retouching, without overdoing it.

The strong highlight on the forehead was softened by *working around it* to left and right. By "stretching" a highlight anywhere on the face, particularly on the forehead, one gives it a better shape and the greasy-skin effect is gone. The technique works on this principle: as a piece of rubber gets thinner as we stretch it or a piece of wool material thinner as one pulls it, so with the highlight. It is only strong because the surrounding area appears darker by contrast. It is well to remember this point. *Retouching is camouflaging,* in a sense. *By subduing one area and slightly strengthening another, we can achieve almost any correction we want.*

No matter how well the retoucher masters the use of the etching knife, he should leave scraping of highlights alone, and should not rely on reducing chemicals. These are fine in commercial or other types of photography, but in portraits are seldom justified.

To return to Fig. 50: after the highlight on the forehead was subdued, other specks on the side of the temple were retouched. Then lines under the eyes were softened with a 2H pencil, and at the same time lines from the mouth to the nose were retouched. These lines are always stronger on a smiling portrait, and one must leave them in, in order to maintain the expression.

The next step is to resume retouching on the center of the cheek where the highlight is strongest. Move the pencil in beamlike fashion (see Fig. 40A) toward the nose, upward to the depression under the eyes, outward to the side of the cheek, and downward to the lower part of the cheek and mouth area. (Imagine a center line running through the earlobes, the tip of the nose, and across the face. This is where one should stop before continuing all the way down the face.)

While retouching on the cheek, extend your retouching stroke beyond the density and work on the shaded rim with tiny, scalloped, up-and-down strokes, which will break up the sharp shadow line. It is not necessary to retouch the rest of the shadow area, because once the rim of a density is subdued the entire shadow area will appear softer.

After the cheek and the side of the face are finished, correct areas above the upper lip between the nose and mouth. Sometimes the nose shadow is not well-defined by studio light and the photographer will request to have it removed. If it is only a light blotch, removing it would be beneficial. However, if it is a strong shadow, the shadow is also repeated on the side of the face and on the shoulders. This light effect is caused by illuminating the sitter with light from above and from the side. Light and shadow must be consistent in a picture and carefully considered by the retoucher. Removing one shadow and leaving another one in would certainly look unnatural. Observe our example, in which the light shadow under the nose was not removed, but only the skin cleared up.

Retouching of the nose is more difficult than it would seem. From observation of photographs in studio windows it is obvious that this is the *least* mastered part of the retoucher's skill. Although the nose contributes no expression to the face, it is still the most individualistic part of a person's features: minute shapes and planes are recorded in that tiny space on the negative, and the retoucher must know accurately how to enhance them.

A skillfully retouched nose gives a portrait a mark of distinction and is the signature of a craftsman. (Observe in all sample illustrations how the nose structure of the face in the photograph shows clear improvement, though the shape of the nose has not been changed.)

The nose has three densities, which the retoucher must learn to recognize. The strongest is the highlight of the bone structure and the tip of the nose. The second density, softer in appearance, denotes the width of the bone. The third, slightly shaded density (particularly in a side-view), is the side or height of the nose, which falls off into the cheeks. The basic approach is applicable to most shapes and poses.

One never does heavy retouching on the nose, yet every little touch should be well-thought-out. Always start on the visible highlight at the bridge of the nose, clean up the section between the eyebrows if it is needed, and work down toward the tip, touching up specks or adding continuity to the highlight. Use strokes No. 1, 3, and 4 to blend around the highlight to establish the width of the nose, moving the pencil more sideways than up-and-down. Cleaning up here and there and making slight corrections on the bridge of the nose, one also defines the shadow line (side of the nose), which sets the nose off from the cheek. If this fine shadow line is not established, the nose will blend into the cheek and give a changed appearance to the face. (There is hardly any separation between the cheeks and nose in babies, which makes their little noses show like "buttons.")

After the nose has been retouched, proceed to the other side of the face, subduing or matching in tone the line under the eye. Always see that both wrinkles under the eyes have the same shape and shade. In a smiling picture the eyes squint, cheeks are raised, and only the *sharpness* of the line should be softened, by an "S" or crescent stroke from the outer corner of the eye. Eyelids are very seldom retouched on younger people, and even on older ones they should be left alone unless change is absolutely necessary.

Continue retouching on the right side of the cheek, being sure not to take out the faint shadow line that indicates the side view of the nose. In the case of Fig. 50 the small dark area on the right side of the nostril was subdued to match the laughline on the other side of the face. Always compare one line against the other, one area against the other, in order not to have any one part too weak or too strong. In this case the small area around the nostril was the darkest part of the illuminated face and needed correction.

Finally, the lines and blemishes from the tip of the chin to the right side of the cheek were retouched to give a better appearance to the model.

NOTE: This is a good practice negative of the average school-type picture. With pencil in hand, try to approximate the finished negative. If you are not satisfied with your practice work, a few drops of spirits of turpentine will remove it. Rub the paper surface gently with a swab of cotton or cleansing tissue. Let it dry, and start again to see whether it can be improved.

Portraits of Mature People

Corrective retouching of portraits of mature men or women requires the ability to discriminate between character lines and

Fig. 51A. Typical portrait of executive. Fig. 51B. Retouched negative. Hairline was evened and light retouching done to subdue lines, while retaining shape of face.

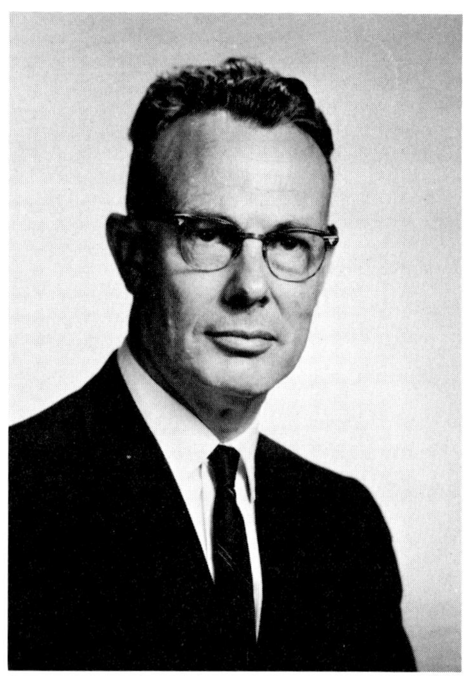

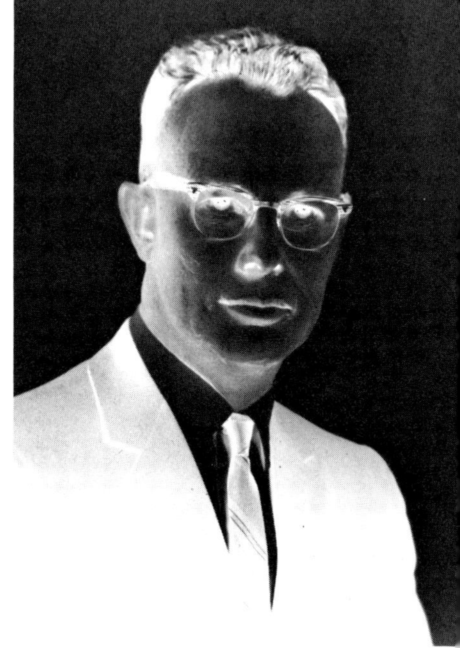

facial defects caused by artificial light, which is never too flattering to people over thirty-five. With practice and observation the retoucher will soon understand where to soften lines, leave them unchanged, or take them out altogether.

However, in my estimation there is no more rewarding work than this particular kind of retouching. Here the retoucher can really show his artistry. He is not confronted so much with tedious texture retouching of school photographs; rather, he can put something in that picture that seems to emanate from within the person, a distinction of character that a young person would probably not have. The face of a mature person, as has been mentioned before, has attained a set expression, caused by years of living, thinking, and feeling. It is all there in the face, and the retoucher sees these invisible elements projected by the expression in the eyes and around the mouth. Fortunate is the retoucher who works for a photographer who "paints pictures with light" because he has a part in that creation. I know of a few retouchers who could earn much more money by doing volume work, but who, out of admiration for the style of a certain photographer, earn much less than they deserve.

The kind of creative retouching we have been discussing is used in "glamour retouching" for publicity, theater, and society clientele, and involves mainly women's portraits. Of course, men of distinction get somewhat similar treatment.

To understand clearly what constitutes the "rejuvenating effect" in salon portraiture, the retoucher can go to the mirror and perform this simple experiment:

Place your thumbs on your jawbone near the ear and with the middle fingers and forefingers pull gently on both sides of the face above the eyebrows near the hairline. As you pull gently you will notice that the jawline appears instantly firmer and the eyebrows rise slightly, thus revealing the secret by which face-lifting is effected. The contour of the face is not changed, but the skin is made tauter. Lines on the forehead and around the mouth and chin become soft and hardly visible.

The actions you have just performed are the massaging motions of beauticians; the five-step retouching method is based on these motions.

Fig. 52A. Positive print from retouched negative. The hairline has been improved in this portrait by etching. Fig. 52B. The retouched negative.

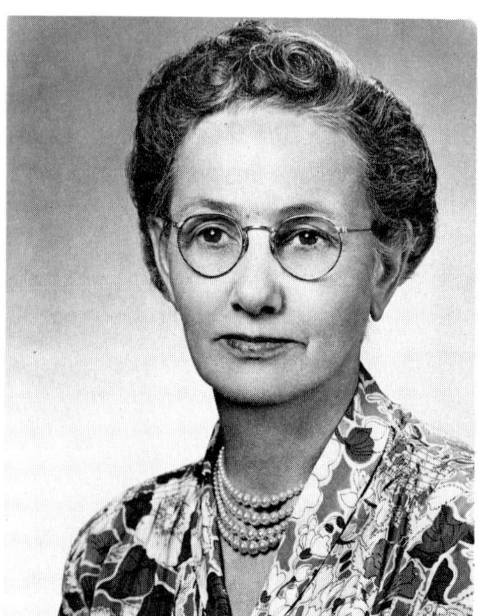

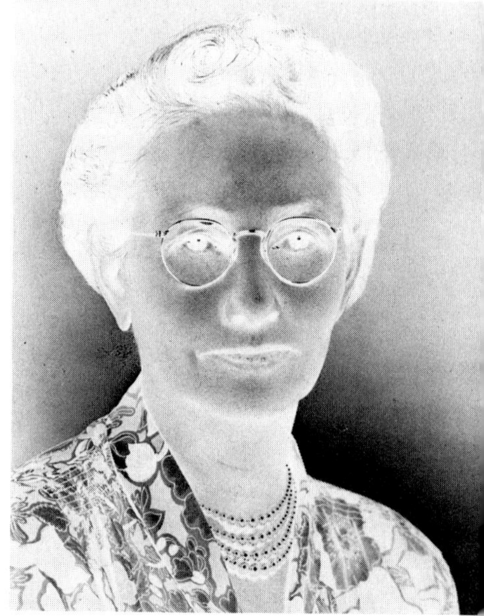

CHAPTER 6

Etching

Background Information on Etching

The word "etching" is not the precise term for this procedure. It should be called "shaving" or "glazing," since the knife is applied with gentle pressure in short or longer swooping strokes on the emulsion side of the negative. By removing the thin layer of silver an effect contrary to that of retouching is produced. Whereas pencil or dye adds density to a negative, the etching knife takes it off (as in cases of hair being added or a neck being made slimmer), leaving a dark area of various degrees on the finished print.

Learning the craft of etching without personal instruction is almost impossible. There are so many pitfalls; the student can keep etching, scraping, digging, fussing with the hold of the knife, not knowing how to keep the knife sharp, etc., until in the end he gives up and tries to do without it.

The art of etching is an indispensable part of the retoucher's technique, and no one can do without it for any length of time. The corrective method of rounding out hairdos, narrowing down protruding cheekbones or thick necks, removing glare from eyeglasses, or adding eyelashes will not be a problem once the retoucher knows how to handle his knife. In good portraiture it is rarely necessary to etch out large parts of the negative, but even a few touches must be done to perfection.

I do not think it is necessary to take a special course to learn how to remove a handkerchief from a breastpocket or open a closed eye, because such corrections will be the natural result of the retoucher's etching skill.

Professional retouchers perform corrections with the etching knife before doping the negative. Once the medium or "dope" is on the negative the surface is coated and the knife does not have the proper grip. Frequently in printing with a condenser-type enlarger the etched area shows up as a lighter density through some peculiar refraction on the negative. If for some reason etching is added *after* dope has been applied, one can re-apply a dab of it and thus seal in the etched part. See for yourself how it shows up in sun-proofing. (Proofs of etched negatives should always be made by the beginner.)

NOTE: On Polaroid negatives the emulsion is very thin, similar to the roll film surface, which makes etching extremely hazardous. If possible, etching should be avoided, unless one is already skilled. The abrading needle (see page 31) is preferable for etching out tiny areas. This is done on the glossy side of the film, mainly with the electric machine.

Whatever etching knife or method the retoucher uses he should beware of overdoing it. With an etching knife in his hand the retoucher becomes at once a hairdresser, dentist, plastic surgeon, and beautician; an artisan whose work demands intelligence and precision.

Ready-Made Etching Knives

Etching knives are delicate instruments, and again one should not spare the expense of buying the best one possible. Some retouchers use only one knife for etching; others use a variety ranging from an engraver's knife to a honed scalpel.

The main problem in purchasing a knife in a camera supply store is that it must be honed. The properly honed knife, kept constantly sharp, already solves about ninety per cent of etching problems. As I have observed in the classroom, the basic skill

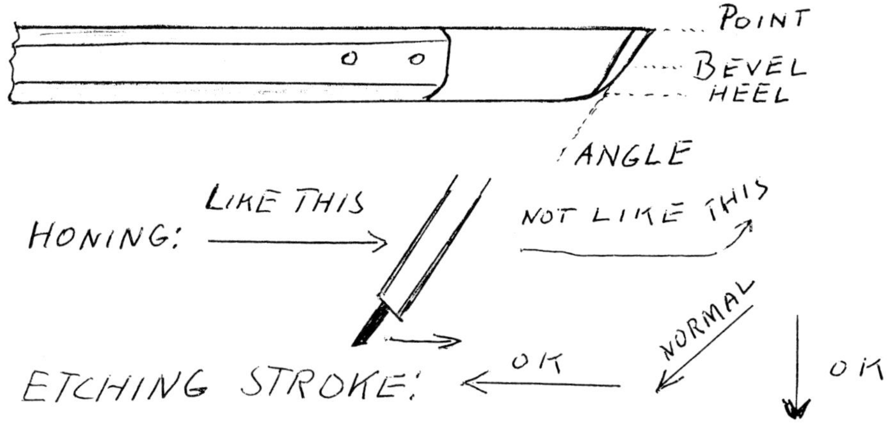

Fig. 53A. Ideal etching knife with indications of honing.

of holding it and working with it can be mastered in a few hours. Very few students have the time or know-how to "set up" the knife in order to get the perfect blade. Each type of commercial etching knife, whether it has a blade that is square or bulky, triangular or thin-pointed, requires a professional honing, an activity that the novice cannot follow even from the description sheet. After the student scratches, digs, and tests, the newly purchased knife ends up in the tool box until some time later, when another make of knife is added to it. Getting discouraged with his attempts, he gives up etching as a lost cause, which it is not.

Bob Forester Ideal Etching Knife

I can recommend only one etching knife, which I have used and demonstrated for many years: the Bob Forester Ideal etching knife. The unique merit and advantage of this knife is its individually pre-honed blade, which never requires "setting up." Included in the purchase price are two sheets of special Behr-Maning 4/0 emery polishing papers. Occasional stropping on this special paper will keep the knife in perfect condition. It might be wise to order additional paper, as this type of jewelry-polishing paper is hard to obtain. Both knife and paper may be

Fig. 53B. Actual honing procedure. Four or five flat stropping strokes across special paper are sufficient to keep knife in good condition. Knife must be moved in one direction only, not back and forth. Therefore it is advantageous to own the pre-honed Ideal etching knife.

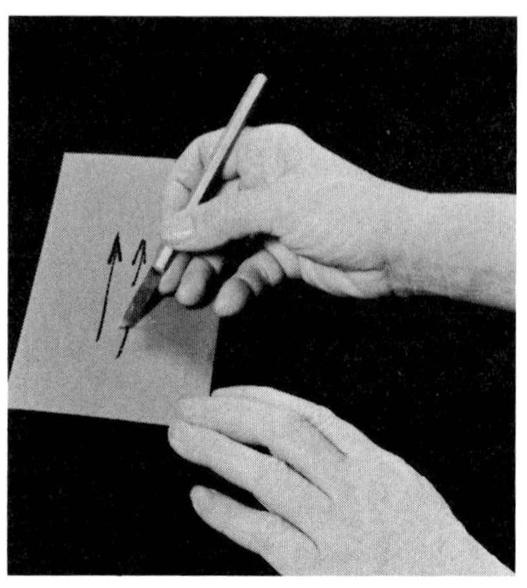

ordered through the National Retouchers Guild, at a price of \$5.50. The jewelry polishing paper is often available in your local lapidary or jewelry repair shop.

NOTE: The etching knife, which is used on negatives, should never be used on prints. The paper, having a rougher surface than film, will destroy the finely-honed edge of the blade. The etching technique that follows further on in this chapter pertains mainly to this knife, but is applicable in general to any other make.

It is up to the individual worker to make the tools perform, but from personal experience I would say that knives sold on the market are of little use to the retoucher who does not know how to set them up, or rather, how to hone them. Honing is indeed a chore.

Honing Procedure

The blade should be slightly tapered and the end angled at about 45°. A bevel is then cut on the edge, either for a right- or left-handed operator. The heel is then rounded and dulled to prevent any accidental cutting. There is a slight rounding of the beveled angle to allow the operator to use the point (on eyelashes, pinholes, fine detail) slightly farther back for general etching, or midway-back for broad etching (reducing highlights, clothing corrections, etc.).

The next step is the most important in the sharpening process. The edge is lightly drawn over the special emery paper. This imparts a microscopic turned edge that would be similar to a miniature carpenter's wood scraper. For this reason *the knife will only cut in one direction.* (Not up and down or back and forth.)

Follow these directions carefully. Place the knife, angled towards you and towards the right, squarely on the beveled edge. Start on the left edge of the emery paper and draw the knife across to the right with a light pressure. Take care to stay directly on the bevel without rocking. (See Fig. 53.)

This sharpening should always be done before starting to etch, and should be done frequently during a heavy session of etching. Etching on paper should not be attempted with this finely-honed knife (more about this in Chapter 8). Directions for sharpening must be reversed for left-handed people, and when ordering a knife you should indicate which hand you favor, so that you get the appropriate directions.

The 4/0 emery polishing paper supplied with the knife will last quite a while before it has to be discarded. I know of no substitute that will work as well.

Etching Technique

The actual method of using the knife can be as individualistic as handwriting. The negative should be laid flat and held securely with the left hand. While etching, keep the negative free of the retouching carrier or mask. It is best to keep one's hand steady, but the negative should be freely turned to suit the direction of the stroke. When using the K. West patented retouching stand, press the mask firmly down to avoid the spring-like action of the disk. (See proper position, Fig. 54.) The knife is held upright and slightly tilted in the direction of the stroke. Some workers draw the knife from right to left, others from top down, or more generally, between the two directions. One should hold the knife as one would hold a pen, the edge of

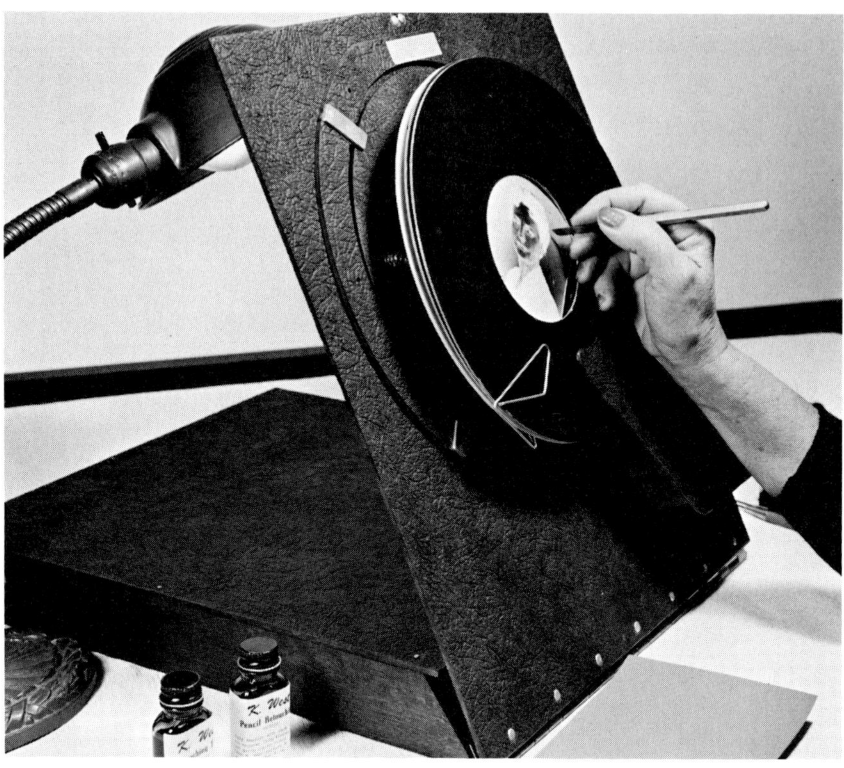

Fig. 54. Holding etching knife. Use inner edge of blade to shave down negative density. Keep turning negative slightly as you make strokes. Keep hand steady, holding knife firmly but applying gently. Turn negative upside down when etching on left side of face.

the blade resting against the first knuckle of the middle finger, the forefinger close to the tip, guiding it, so to speak. The etching stroke is softest at a fraction beyond the bevel, the blade turned slightly to the right, but the finger action moving to the left. Never have the heel of the blade turned against the face. Turn the negative upside down when etching on the left side of the head.

The stroke should be so gentle and light that only after several "shaving" motions does the negative show transparency. With a light steady motion from the wrist, let the knife touch the surface in mid-motion, till you observe the silver dust or

Fig. 55. (I) Wrong etching stroke; (II and III) gradually intensified soft etching stroke; (IV) stroke for etching hair or curved lines; (V) straight stroke on down movement.

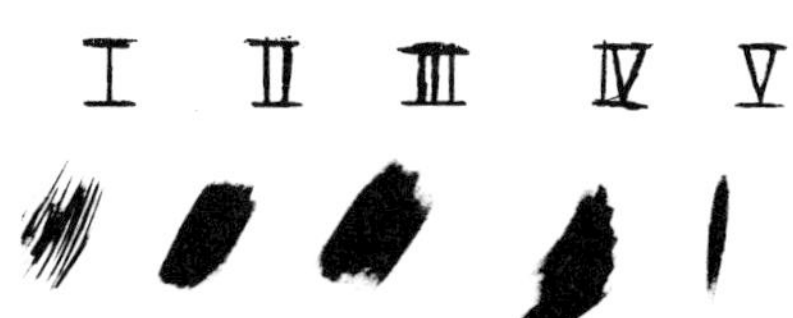

shaving of the negative. If it comes in heavy curled streaks you are etching too heavily. Practice on the background and try several positions of knife and fingers till you see smooth, soft areas. Figure 55 shows the right and wrong etching stroke.

Once you have familiarized yourself with holding the knife properly you will observe that the heel will make broad strokes, and holding the knife almost perpendicular to the negative you will achieve tiny areas of sharp lines. A test stroke should always be made before starting, no matter how long you have been etching. Have a discarded negative on hand, or in an emergency try the extreme corner of the negative. Once you have established the stroke you need, apply the blade to the area to be etched without changing the position of your grip.

As was mentioned before, sun proofs are of great help in judging the results of etching. If an area seems darker than the surrounding part of the negative, dye and pencil will correct it sufficiently to improve it. If the etched area appears too light, further etching must be done. There should be no trace of density separation in good etching, nor should the retoucher have to resort to corrective methods with dye or pencil. The retoucher should not become discouraged. It takes just the first few soft strokes of etching to give him a grasp of the techniques. From then on it is just a matter of practice.

NOTE: Keep the negative clean. Brush off shavings as you go along, with tissue paper or the back of your little finger or by blowing them off. (This is another reason why I like etching before doping. The silver dust never gets stuck to the negative.) Etching to fill out a hairline is the easiest way to learn the etching strokes.

Do not drag the knife over the negative with a stiff motion. Always make short and then longer strokes, and do not stay too long on one spot. When working on a hairline, outline it first with a soft stroke and then begin etching from the hairline to the outside part to be filled in.

Etching should also have gradation in tone. One must think in reverse, so to speak—deeper or more numerous strokes where there would be a shade of hair, lighter or fewer where part of the hair has a highlight. (With soft pencil one can add sharper highlight effects when part of the etched hair seems to lack detail.)

A pebbly effect on an etched area indicates that the knife is dull or that it is being held too far back. In good etching the hairline should have a soft outline. Compare with the general outline of the head and observe that the hairline never is as sharply defined, but gives a feeling of space behind it. Sharp edges on a hairdo make the head look like a cutout.

Keep the knife firmly between the fingers and do not let it slip around. The rule for etching is: *The grip should be firm, the touch gentle.*

Etching on Eyes

The eyes, eyebrows, and eyelids are of such importance in preserving the likeness and expression of a person that it is advisable to leave corrections on these areas for final print spotting.

Where more than one catchlight gives the eye a glassy expression, one catchlight may be removed with the tip of the knife or the abrading needle. The catchlight appears as a round, dark spot on the negative. The one in the center of the pupil should be removed for a softer expression.

CHAPTER 7

Dye Retouching

General Information on Dye Retouching

Working with negative dye is nothing new. Different types of dye have been used for years by photographers, here and abroad. Application, however, has been kept at a minimum, because it always seemed an intricate and difficult technique that only a few could master. Although some retouchers have learned to work with dyes by now, it is hoped that eventually every retoucher will consider the dye retouching method. It is of the utmost importance to the photographic profession.

Pencil retouching has its limitations: large areas are tedious and sometimes impossible to retouch with pencil to the desired density. Modern photography tends toward thin negatives and sharp texture tone, and only a minimum of pencil retouching will be effective on this type of negative. There is no better way to retouch wrinkles, lines, and blemishes than the precise pencil application, but dye retouching can take care of almost sixty per cent of the total work required for a first-class job. It is not only suitable as a substitute for pencil work, but is also the finest method of spotting prints, either glossy or matte. Dye can be used for retouching separation negatives and for dye transfers. It will give a perfect base for color dye on color transparencies. It solves almost every problem of photographic retouching. Visual proof of the effectiveness of dye retouching can be found in Fig. 56.

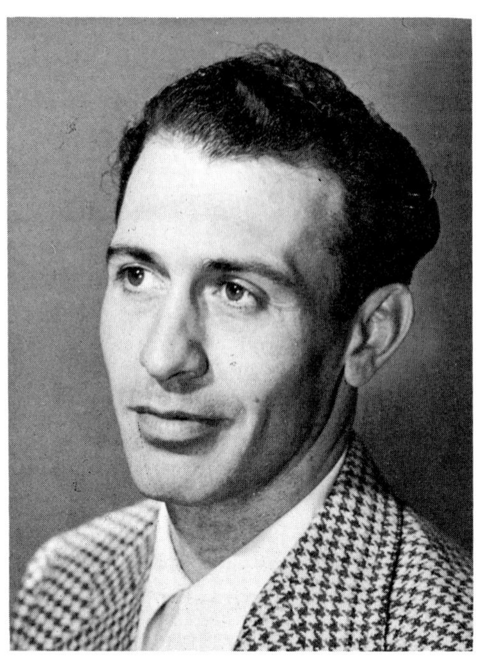

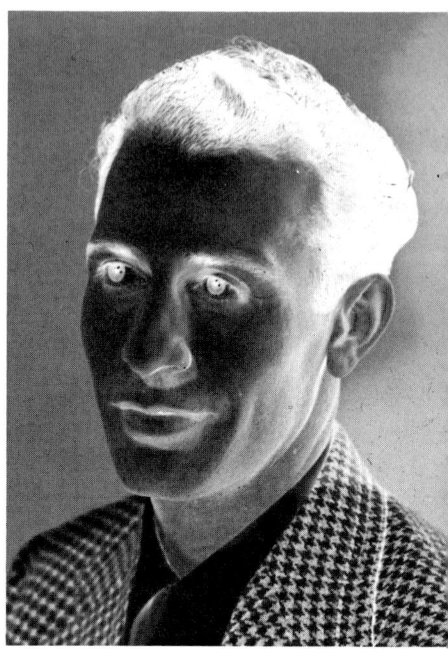

Fig. 56A (Above, left). Ideal negative density for dye work. Positive print from unretouched negative. Fig. 56B (Above, right). Unretouched negative. Soft or normal negative is most gratifying for dye retouching with ready-mixed K. West Dye. Sometimes 70 per cent of retouching can be done in a few minutes. Fig. 56C (Below, left). Print from dye-retouched negative. Fig. 56D (Below, right). On this negative not a single stroke of pencil was applied, yet it has appearance of retouched portrait.

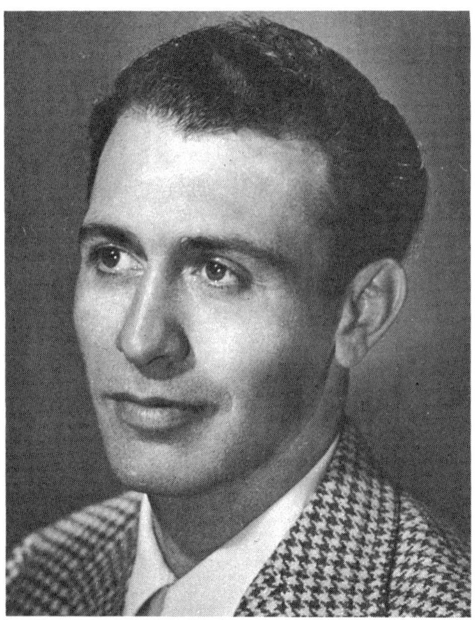

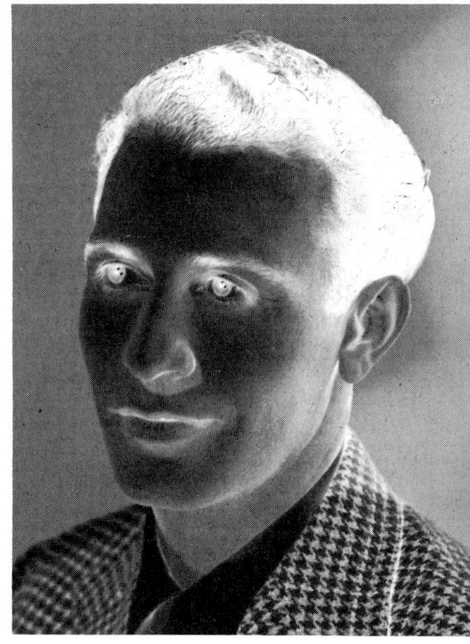

Dye retouching will be particularly helpful to the amateur, because perfection can be achieved much faster, and improvement in work made more apparent; it is thus more gratifying than any other medium. You may wonder, then, why I have gone into pencil retouching in detail in previous chapters. It is simply because anyone mastering pencil retouching can quickly adapt himself to dye retouching. Since dye work is similar in motion and tonal quality to pencil work, eyes and hands already trained to treating density gradations in negatives will have little difficulty in combining both techniques.

NOTE: When you are using the dye, the negative should be held outside the negative carrier or mask. To prevent any fingerprints on the negative while handling it, cut a corner from an envelope and hold the negative with it. This is also recommended when etching. All instructions in this book are for the All Purpose Dye (K. West Retouching Dye), because it is the only ready formulated dye that simplifies the dye application techniques explained in the following pages. Additional brands are also mentioned for those retouchers who wish to mix their own dyes.

Equipment

1 bottle of All Purpose Dye
1 No. 000 sable brush
1 No. 00 sable brush
1 swab or tiny sponge

The important factor in successful dye work is the brush, a subject we have already discussed in Chapter 2, "Retouching Equipment."

K. West Dye

After testing a number of dyes available on the market, I found that great skill was required in diluting them, which is a rather time-consuming task, not to mention that diluted dyes give dubious results in corrected areas. After conducting tests on every type of negative, I formulated in 1945 the K. West

Retouching Dye, now under the name of All Purpose Dye.

The advantages of the K. West Dye are:

1. It is of a neutral gray tone, whether viewed by transmitted or reflected light.

2. It needs no dilution for use on negatives, only slight thinning for print spotting when the lightest tone of gray is required.

3. It blends evenly into the gelatin surface, resembling the density of a medium pencil, which can gradually be increased by one application over another.

4. It is a fast dye that does not change color even when exposed to light.

5. It does not evaporate and will leave no residue in the bottle.

6. It is soluble in water, allowing for correction of any mistake by washing the negative under water.

7. It has an absolute transparent quality, even at its strongest density.

8. It is a perfect spotting color for all photographic papers.

In addition to the ready-mixed K. West Dye, there are other retouching and spotting dyes available that are useful. Spotone, Dyene, Marshall, and Webster dyes are available for the retoucher and spotter who will take the time and trouble to make them suitable for his own technique.

NOTE: Close bottles of dye or medium immediately after you are through with them. Many bottles get spilled on the retouching table when they are left open and knocked over in the dark. The bottom part of an egg carton is a most practical way to hold bottles of dye. Cut off the tip of the egg-shaped carton so that the bottles sit securely in the grooves. The top part of the carton can be used for laying out pencil and brushes and other paraphernalia. Try it.

Brush Technique

To acquire a feel for the brush technique, practice first on

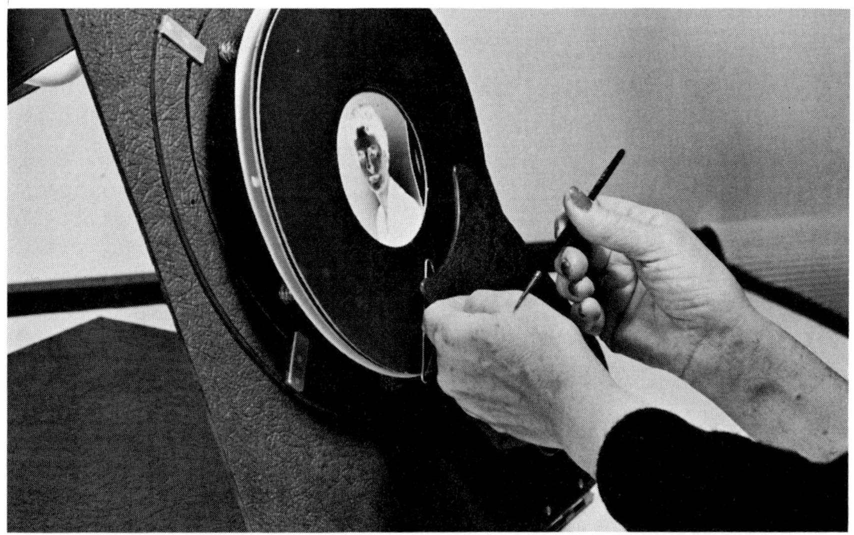

Fig. 57. The author's method of removing excess dye from brush. Stroke brush twice flatly over side of hand near thumb. I get a perfect point and a moist brush. It may be unorthodox, but I have been doing it this way for 20 years (with K. West Dye).

discarded negatives. Practice dye application on shadows from folds, background, or objects on the negative before attempting it on the face.

Learn to apply the dye sparingly, wiping the brush flatly across the back of the left hand once or twice to take off any excess (Fig. 56). This is preferable to wiping it on blotting paper, as it forms a perfect point and leaves the brush moist —not dry. It is to be expected that the beginner will be heavy-handed and will make blotches at first instead of soft, even areas. A slight discoloration of the negative will show where too much dye has been deposited. It is not a serious mistake. When a sun-proof is made, it will be seen that the discoloration has almost no effect in printing value. The feel for the proper amount of dye application will come with practice. As in all things, practice makes perfect.

The trick in dye retouching as well as in pencil work is to secure the desired density by repeated applications of thin

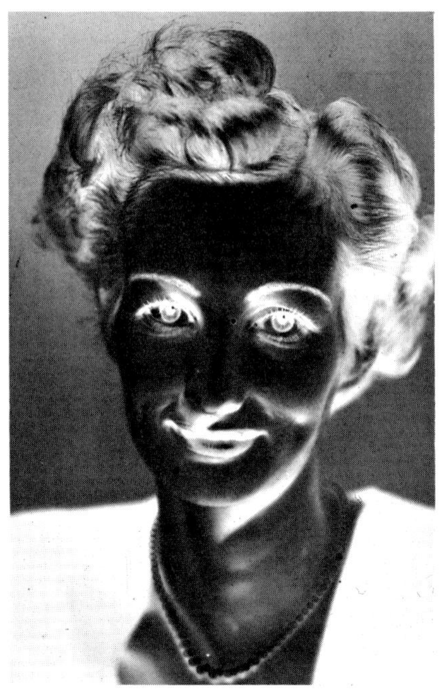
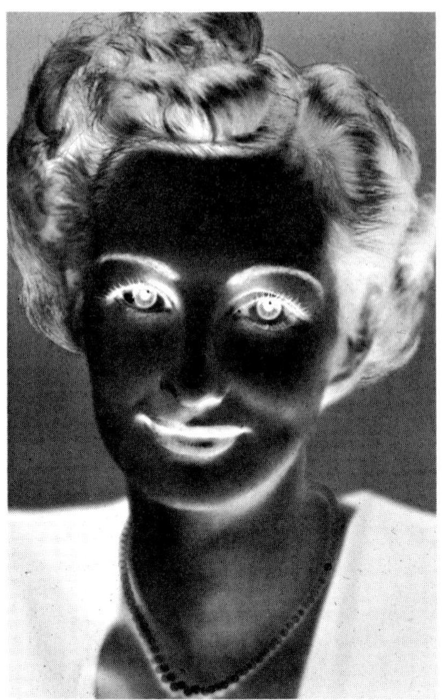

Fig. 58A (Left). Case of extensive retouching correction. Indicates that retoucher skilled with etcher, dye, and pencil can, in an emergency, turn out a saleable picture. (This one was a discard.) In this picture, nose looks too long, cheeks cast unbecoming lines and shadows. Shadow on neck elongates face still more. Hair is unflatteringly arranged. Fig. 58B (Right). Drastically changed picture with all possible correction. Without dye application it would have been impossible to soften shadows as much. With sunken-in area of cheeks retouched, face appears wider, jawline firmer and slightly rounder on right side of face. Sharp highlight on nose was softened with pencil retouching only, lightening density around highlight to reduce it. Finally, some hair was added near left side of face to eliminate ragged contour.

layers, rather than by a single heavy stroke with a loaded brush.

The effect of dye will be quickly noticed as you work, first of all in the folds of clothing. The dye is an intensifier, bringing out the texture of the material, which is nearly invisible in the shadow density. Work with deliberation, moving the brush evenly. Never bear down on it as you would in painting. The touch should be so light that the tip of the brush does not bend under the pressure of the hand. Dye-retouching cannot be compared to any other brush technique. The experimental stage will be shortened by many hours if this important point is kept in mind.

MOISTENING THE NEGATIVE

A wet swab of lightly squeezed-out absorbent cotton or a tiny sponge should *always* be at your side. Moistening of the area where work is to be done will help at first, because the water slightly softens the gelatin and will give more even blending.

When dye application does not conform to the desired density, it can be reduced to a mere shade by washing the negative under a gentle flow of tap water for a few minutes. Inspect it from time to time against the light to see how much the areas are subdued. Hang up the negative to dry. For those retouchers who do not have negative hangers, the following suggestion may be helpful: hold the negative at the upper left-hand corner and use a small spring clothespin to grasp it. Only the transparent border of the film should be clasped, never the film emulsion. Attach a piece of string to the clothespin and hang the negative so that it does not lean against or touch any object. If it touches anything, it will curl up and dry unevenly.

As one advances in the brush technique, moistening of small areas will not often be necessary. The advantage of the dry method lies in the fact that details of modeling and retouching on the face remain crisp and clear. Hold the brush as if it were a pencil, perpendicular to the negative. Keep the density rather "underdone" with tiny doodling motions that overlap evenly.

The negative must be completely dry before it is turned over to the matte side for pencil retouching. Otherwise the moist gelatin will stick to the glass plate and may peel off, leaving a ruined negative. Pencil retouching takes care of pulling tones together and applying a textured effect.

If both sides of the negative are used for removing deep lines, all dye work should be finished before the retouching medium is applied. Dye retouching cannot be done over a doped negative, as the layer of thin varnish prevents it from penetrating into the emulsion. Only carbon tetrachloride or benzene will remove retouching medium to make the negative once more receptive to dye work.

The more one works with dye retouching, the more the speed of its effects is noticeable. Attention has purposely been called to the difficulties experienced by the beginner so that he will not be disappointed over his first try. The reader may get the impression that dye procedure is rather complex, but this is really not so. Considering that only a few strokes of the brush overcome deep shadows, which in pencil retouching would take much longer and perhaps show roughness on a print, the initial patience, study, and practice are worth the effort. Once the skill of dye retouching is mastered, a retoucher will wonder how he ever got along without it. As you will see in Figs. 58 and 59, skillful dye retouching can vastly improve an unflattering portrait, and make an unsaleable picture saleable.

NOTE: Sometimes the dye does not readily penetrate the emulsion of a negative. This may be due to dirt or special acid-hardening fixatives used in developing the negative. The remedy is to rub the negative down gently with a swab soaked in carbon tetrachloride or benzene, till it is dry. Often a piece of cotton that has been soaked in water and squeezed out will suffice to soften the hard gelatin surface.

Remedies for Common Dye Retouching Mistakes

In retouching with dye, as with any other retouching method, the retoucher should know how to correct his own mistakes. Here, then, are the common faults in dye retouching, and the remedy for each:

SMALL DARK BLOTCHES

The brush should be applied in mid-motion, not set straight on the negative. Keep it moving with a continuous tiny stroke, building up gradually to desired density. About three or four strokes are necessary before a change of shade is visible. The retoucher has to keep in mind that he should use the brush as he would a pencil (a liquid pencil so to speak) and make the same tiny strokes, overlapping and intensifying them gradually.

CLOUDY EFFECT (Uneven Application in Large Area)

Moisten negative *before* using the swab with dye. Move in loose ovals or circles in a rather quick motion around the spot where dye is already strong. Blend edges but do not overlap into the dense area.

DARK STREAKS (Caused by Dust Specks in Brush or Dry Brush)

Apply moist cotton swab immediately to take off heavy streak. If necessary, wash negative under faucet. *Never put finger on moist negative. Never use dry cotton to remove speck while working with dye.*

BLISTERS ON NEGATIVE (Too Much Wetting Causes Softening of Gelatin)

Lay negative to one side and let dry until all trace of moisture has disappeared. Dab gently with moist cotton to avoid blistering.

DULL SPOTS ON GLOSSY SIDE (Caused by Heavy Soaking of Cotton Swab)

When negative is completely dry, apply retouching medium over glossy side to restore sheen.

One mistake should be avoided from the beginning. The very fine lines on the forehead or other parts of the face and neck should not be removed with the brush unless they show

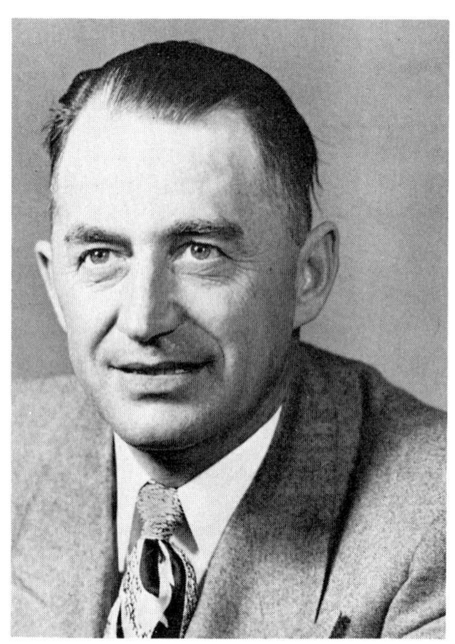

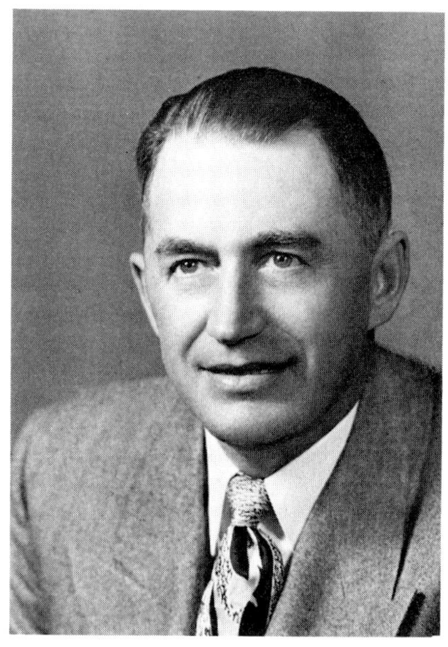

Fig. 59A. Portrait of older man. Dye was applied to right side of face where cheek highlight dips without gradation into shadow. Lines under eyes need softening. Fig. 59B. Retouched print. Notice how softened shadow on shoulder at right, done with dye on swab, brings out texture of material. After dye work, only light texture retouching was necessary to preserve man's skin texture. Blister and rough skin under nose needed even tone. Light specks near blister were touched up on print. Observe corrected hairline, which always improves a portrait. Older people do not have their pictures taken frequently, so they do not mind looking a few years younger.

up as a soft density or are wide enough for the tip of the brush to take out the narrow line without overlapping its edges. The dye has the tonal value of a hard pencil, which in itself would not be strong enough to take out heavy lines. If the brush is too broad for the line, white streaks will show up on the print. By avoiding such mistakes at first, your dye retouching will satisfy you as well as the most discriminating photographer.

Dye Retouching Technique on Portraits

1. Place negative on retouching stand, glossy side up.

2. Dip brush in bottle of dye, then wipe over back of left hand.

3. Start on forehead, *working from strongest density* to left and right. When forehead has no pronounced highlight, start on temple and, holding negative sideways, work along in horizontal direction.

4. Retouch shadow under eye lightly, but skip wrinkles.

5. Strengthen highlight on nose, but keep it soft.

6. Retouch on left side of face in the manner already explained in Chapter 4 under "Systematic Retouching."

7. Proceed to right side of face, starting from cheekbone, balancing or blending highlights into the adjoining halftones or shadows.

8. With tiny scalloped strokes, retouch strong smile lines or furrows from nostrils to mouth, being careful not to take them out altogether. One can remove a wrinkle from a face, but density must be added on the cheek to keep the ratio of facial form unchanged.

9. Start on center of chin (Step 5) and move brush with upward strokes to the left and right along the jawline. If there is no contrast in density between face and neck, add density along jawline until contrast appears.

10. Work on shadows on neck, skipping deep lines. Application of dye in wide creases will give a good base on which to do additional pencil retouching. A finely pointed swab is ideal

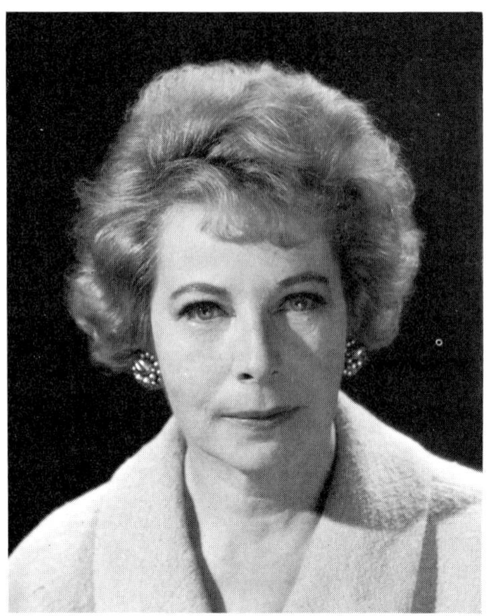

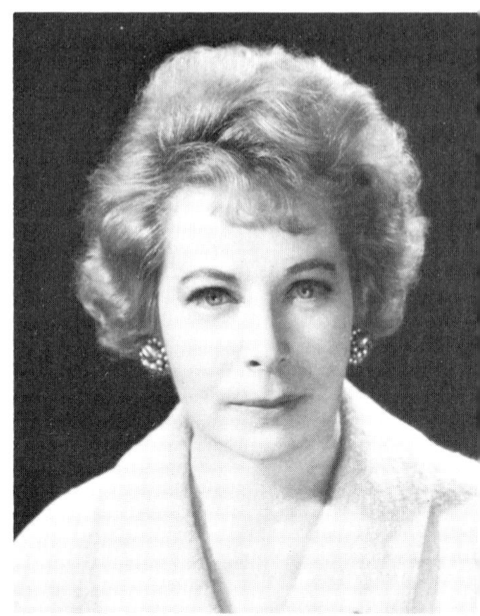

Fig. 60A. Example of how an entire part of face can be lightened without eliminating contrast of light and shadow. Fig. 60B. Dye was applied with finely-pointed swab over areas on face, neck, and shoulder. Also, shadows along neckline and on coat were lightened to give subtler gradation. Additional retouching with pencil was done on face and neck. Pupil on right eye was enlarged to remove starry catchlight.

for shadowy parts of face and neck. It makes soft areas without streaks. (See Fig. 60.)

A hairline requiring more detail should be worked with curved strokes, indicating the natural wave. Separate highlights can be picked out with a 2B pencil. A few short and a few longer strokes in close succession will give the hair a glossy appearance. This is particularly appropriate for women's hair.

When a few modifications on the face and neck are to be made, dye retouching with K. West Dye alone will be sufficient. Fig. 61 is a good example of what dye retouching can do for these areas.

Dye retouching has become a must for the modern retoucher who wants to stay in business and has to keep up with progress in photography. The all-around use of the K. West Dye lies in

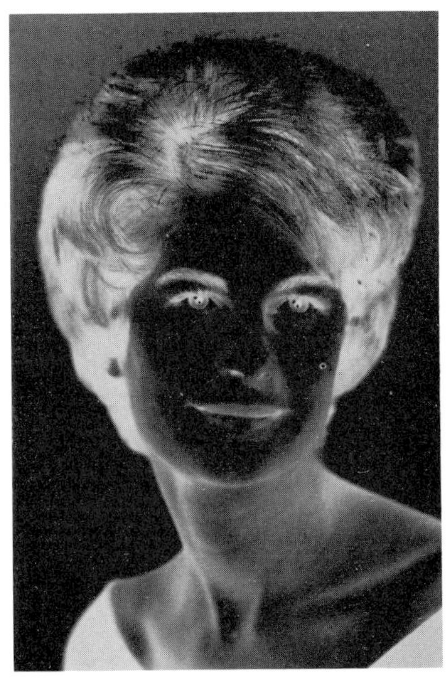

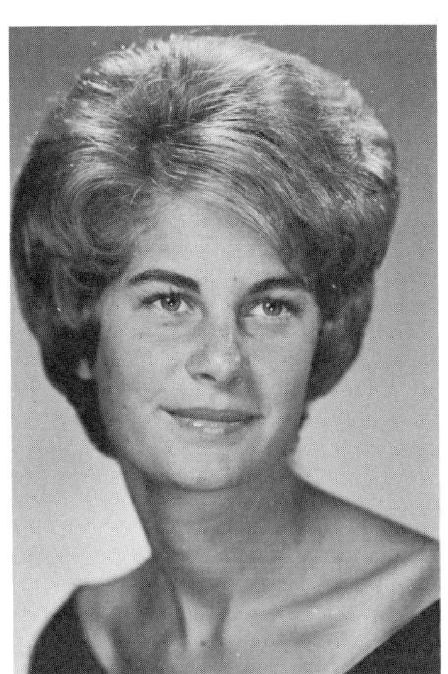

Fig. 61A (Above, left). Example of stages of retouching. Unretouched negative. Fig. 61B (Above, right). Unretouched print. Fig. 61C (Right). Indicates where dye was applied.

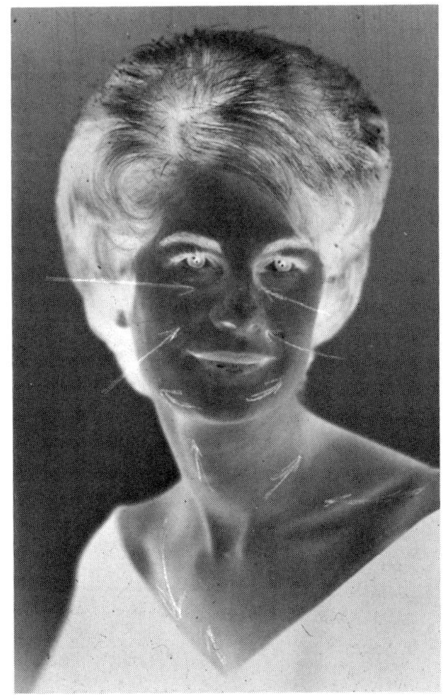

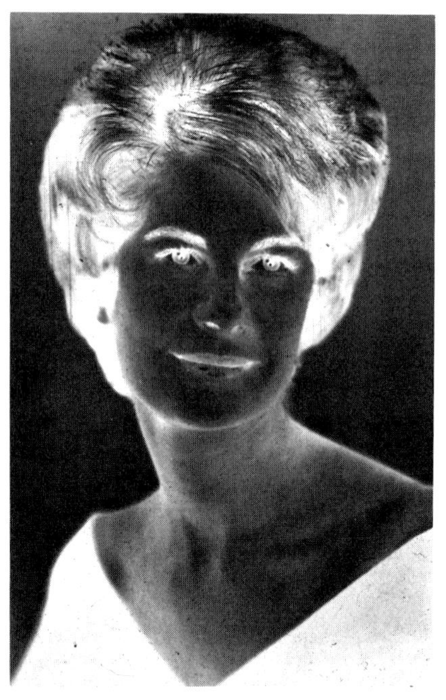

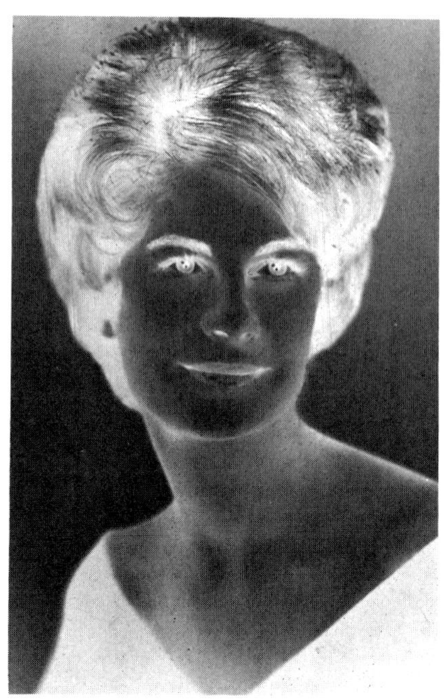

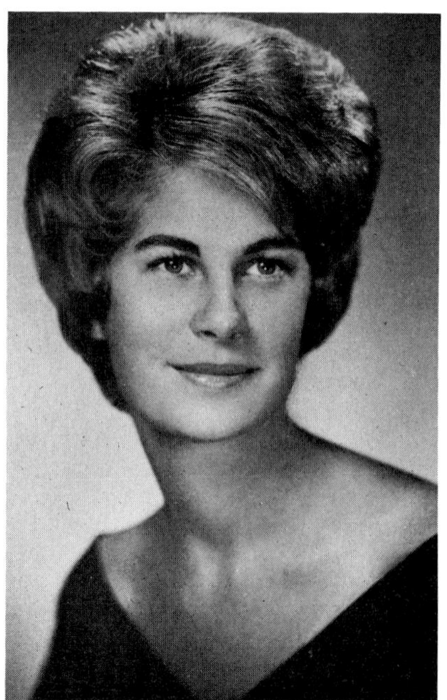

Fig. 61D (Above, left). Negative with dye retouching only. Fig. 61E (Above, right). Retouched negative with added pencil work. Fig. 60F (Left). Finished print.

the fact that it is also suitable for color film and color print retouching. The retoucher who has experience in working with the dye on black-and-white negatives will have no trouble using the technique in color work. This will be explained in Chapter 11.

NOTE: In the first stages of dye retouching, the beginner should use dye very sparingly on the face. There is a tendency for the novice to "paint" the face, because the translucency of the dye is misjudged. Remember that dyes *should be worked in areas for blending and softening, rather than in lines or on skin texture.* Once this technique is mastered, the combination of pencil and dye will result in a picture of the finest quality a retoucher can produce.

Other Uses of Dye

RETOUCHING ROLL FILM

Roll film or any other type of film (70mm, Polaroid, etc.) that has a delicate, thin emulsion is not easy to retouch with pencil. Dye retouching will prove to be a very convenient way to correct small or large areas. A No. 000 brush is to be used when working on tiny areas, but blemishes and fine lines are better taken care of with an application of a very soft pencil (HB, B, or 2B). The retouching is done at very close range with the magnifying glass, and the negative often becomes clouded or even curls slightly from warm breath or the heat from the light bulb below. It should be pointed out that the patented K. West retouching stand has a particular advantage in this respect. The double mask, pivoted at one point, may be separated in order to allow the smallest opening for a film. On the other hand, a 5″ x 7″ negative may be viewed by pushing the double disk to the side.

Roll film in strips can be placed in an envelope with an opening cut out large enough to expose one frame. This will help to hold the strip and prevent finger marks on the delicate surface. Color film can be handled in the same manner.

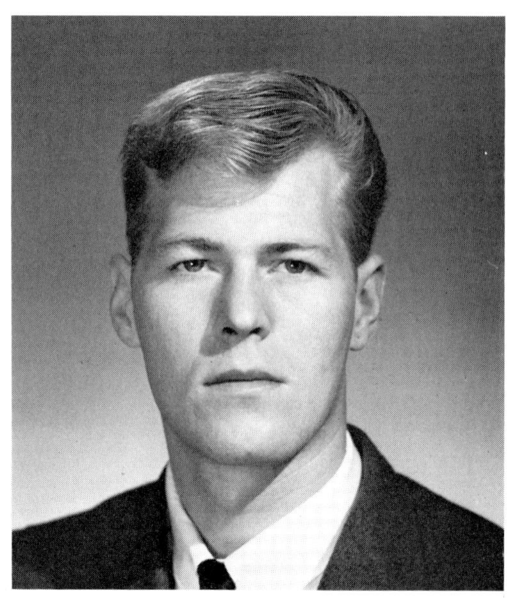

Fig. 62A. Unretouched portrait with deep shadow in forehead that can only be subdued with dye retouching. Fig. 62B. Retouched print shows great improvement and still retains the feel of the original lighting without disturbing shadows.

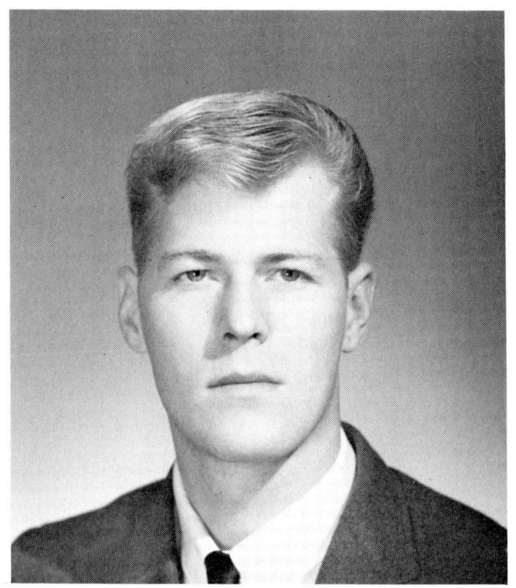

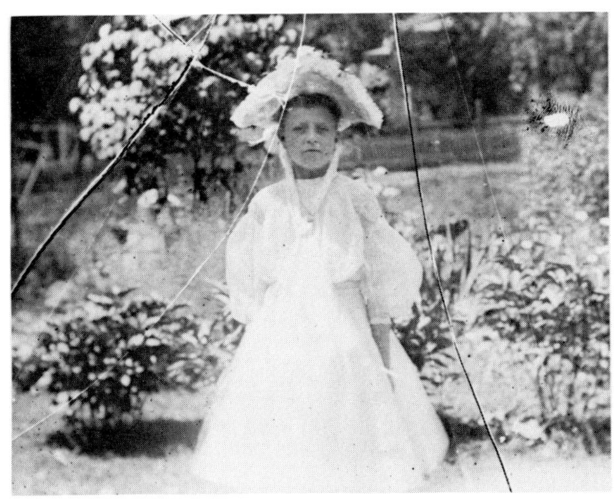

Fig. 62C (Above). This print was made from a broken glass negative, and then dye was applied in all light areas. The print was sprayed with matte lacquer to allow additional work with various tones of grey-color lead pencils (Eagle Prisma-Color) in order to camouflage cracks and large spot on right side. In areas where paper was no longer absorbent, another coat of lacquer was applied to get a good print for a copy negative. Fig. 62D (Below). The copy negative from the near perfect print was then carefully retouched for spots on dress, face, and other parts of background. The very fine light cracks were previously filled in with regular graphite and additional spotting was done on final matte print.

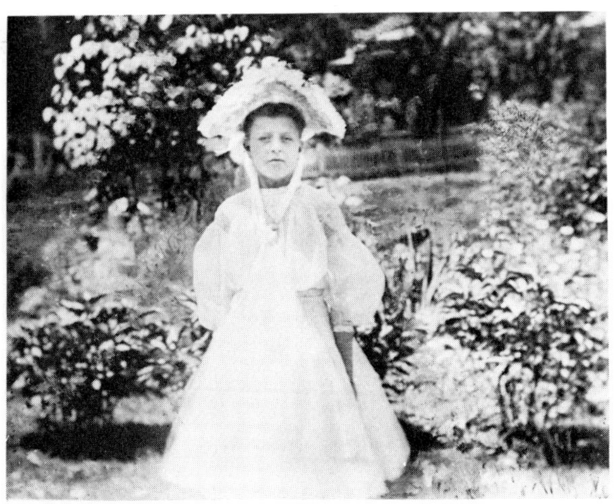

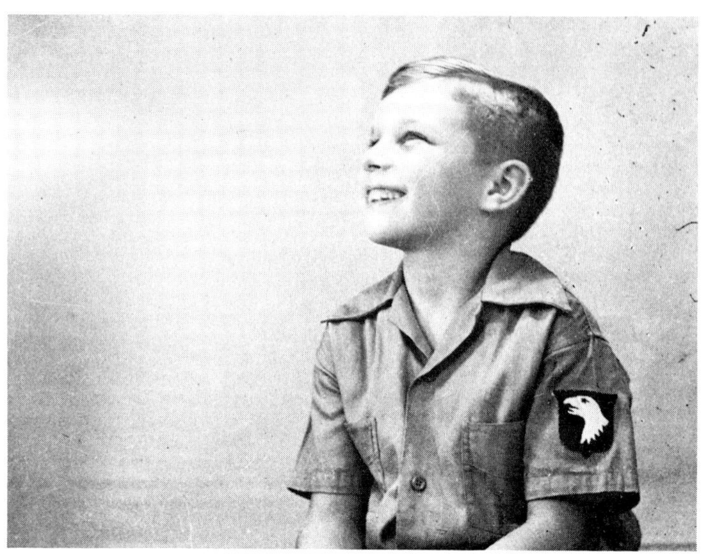

Fig. 62E. Here is another example of how to improve an old, scratched photograph. Fig. 62F. Instead of opaquing out the background, a little oil color was applied over the copy print to make the background more interesting. (See Chapter 9.) The use of opaque oil covers for background changes is becoming increasingly important in color print correction. The method is the same as black-and-white prints, but the colors differ. (See Chapter 12.)

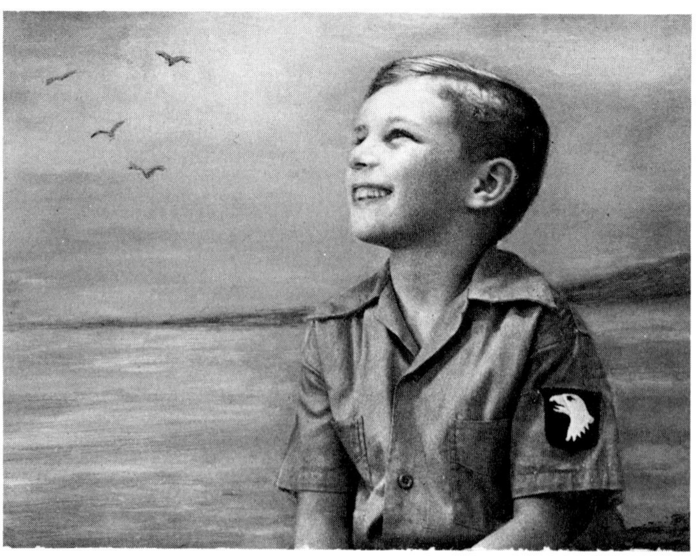

RESTORING OLD PHOTOGRAPHS

Dye retouching can correct and improve old photographs. Formerly, airbrush was considered the only technique that would do a good job. The dye procedure is faster and less costly to the photographer than airbrush work, which can be handled only by skilled craftsmen who charge accordingly. Fig. 62 shows the astonishing results that can be achieved in restoring an old photograph by means of dye retouching.

Procedure: Clean the original photograph carefully with spirits of turpentine or carbon tetrachloride to remove imbedded dust and grime. Dilute a few drops of dye in a small dish or bottle cap and apply it with a *moist* brush to all parts of the picture that need a better delineation: hair, eyebrows, eyes, lips, shadows of clothes, frills, etc. This correction of the original print takes only a few minutes, but it helps greatly in getting a stronger copy negative.

Old photographs often show cracks and light blotches. These defects can be eliminated by retouching the print with a hard pencil, filling them in to match the tones of the surrounding areas. If the applied pencil or dye does not match the stronger or slightly different shade of paper, it should not cause concern, because all tones can be evened or blended again on the copy negative. Subduing an overstrong area on the copy negative is much simpler than not having enough detail to work on.

When the copy negative is made, proceed to the regular retouching of skin texture, which is always grainy on copy negatives. The coarse texture of the photographic print produces this grain in reproduction. Details of highlights should be strengthened wherever possible, but on the other hand the soft, mellow effect of old-time photography should be preserved.

In the chapter on "Print Retouching and Spotting," steps to improve an old print will be further explained.

RETOUCHING NEGATIVE FAULTS

Pinholes: The simplest medium for covering larger pinholes is the opaque spotting color or liquid opaque color without dilution. The K. West Dye is *not* suitable for this purpose. The tiny holes devoid of emulsion need a stronger filling medium. In many instances the abrading needle of the electric retouching machine or electric Porta Point pencil is used to scrape the glossy side and diffuse the pinhole to such an extent that it becomes hardly visible. Also, the tip of the etching knife will produce a similar effect. A 2B pencil is used on either side to deposit enough graphite to cover the pinhole completely.

The technique with spotting colors is as follows: Moisten brush with saliva (the best adherent) and remove a little color from the spotting disk. With the tip of the brush apply a tiny dot in the center of the pinhole, using the magnifying glass for better viewing. Spotting color can be applied to both sides of the negative if the pinhole does not absorb enough at one application. The *brush must be almost dry,* otherwise the color runs over the edge of the pinhole, forming a ring that will make it worse than before. The spotting will show up on the print as a white mark, but dye or pencil will correct it easily right on the print. One can also take the etching knife and *gently scrape the overloaded pinhole area* on the negative to conform as much as possible to the negative density.

Air Bubbles: Air bubbles appear as lighter blots on the negative and are quite easy to retouch. The area can be intensified with a few touches of the dye to match the surrounding density. Also, pencil may be used to blend marginal lines or touch up minute details.

Scratches: Products sold in photo supply stores to remedy scratches usually give satisfactory results. Sometimes an application of retouching medium will sufficiently overcome the negative defect, if the scratch is on the *glossy* side. The pencil is the safest and most reliable way to disguise a scratch when it is on the *emulsion* side. There is no substitute for pencil retouching when one has to correct a scratch extending over varied densities. When the scratch appears as a dark line on the negative, it must be taken care of with either the abrading needle or the tip of the etching knife. Often a good spotting on the print will be much simpler and easier for matching the tones of printing paper.

The retoucher who understands the fundamental techniques of pencil and dye-retouching can apply his experience to all correction in his own way once he has learned through experience what should be left for spotting and how much can be corrected on the negative.

Fingerprints: These are caused by carelessly touching the negative during development of the film in the darkroom. The natural oil of the skin adheres to the film surface, preventing the developing solution or fixative from penetrating. Fingerprints usually show up in the background and can be subdued or overcome altogether by stippling dye in the light area and making additional corrections with pencil.

When finger marks are caused by handling the negative at the retouching stand, a good rubbing with tissue paper on the *glossy side* will make it shine. If finger imprints are also visible on the emulsion (dull) side, apply a dab of medium and blend down gently. A retoucher should inspect every negative for finger marks before handing it over for printing. Regardless of whether a machine or hand-operated retouching stand is used, at some time or other the retoucher handles the negative. To avoid unnecessary work and complaints by the photographer, do not forget to use the corner of the envelope to guard against finger marks.

Background Effects

BLURRING BUSY BACKGROUND

When the photographer has no choice of background or backdrop, it may be necessary to point up the subject by retouching busy details in the background. The procedure is the simplest technique of dye retouching.

Application: Wrap a small piece of absorbent cotton over the tip of a wooden skewer. Make sure the tip is covered so that the negative will not be damaged by an exposed point.

Work in large interlocking strokes from the *rim of the negative* toward the main subject. Keep the swab almost parallel to the negative to get a wide, flat area of shade. Keep the negative moist with the sponge or swab, avoiding vigorous motions or pressure on the film. Repeat the application again and again so that the dye will be absorbed evenly by the film surface. Slow movements will hasten the procedure. The dye will blur the sharp outline of objects to such an extent that they remain only slightly visible. The advantage of blurring the background is that it creates a softness that gives a feeling of distance and makes the foreground objects stand out.

When, after seeing a sun proof, you decide the result is not satisfactory, wash the negative under the faucet or soak it for a while in a dish of water to which a few drops of ammonia have been added. All dye work will be removed without damage to the negative. However, be sure to let the negative get absolutely *dry* before making another sun proof or repeating an application. It intensifies only if successive layers of dye are dried and others applied over it. Also, the emulsion side of the negative will take dye for blurring the background. If a small detail has to be retouched with pencil, apply retouching medium to one or both sides, but make certain that each surface is dry. *Do not touch* moist surface with the fingers! Reread: "Remedies for Common Dye Retouching Mistakes," page 99.

NOTE: For more intense blurring of background or "dodging work," "Dyene" (Retouch Methods Co.) is an excellent product to have on hand. Instructions are included with the three bottle set and should be followed carefully.

TEST FOR VARIOUS PORTRAIT BACKGROUND EFFECTS

Before working directly on the portrait and not being sure if the particular effect appeals to you, try it out on a glassine envelope, fixed-out film, or clear negative the size of the negative. Tape the film and negative together. First wet swab slightly in water and then immerse it in dye. This will prevent your

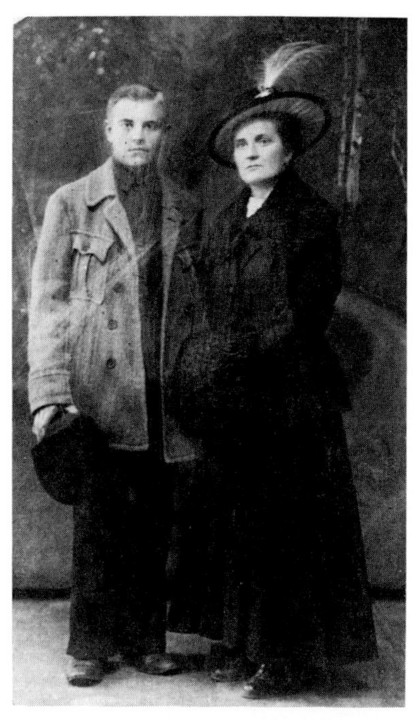

Fig. 63A. There are two ways a retoucher can remove one person from a photograph: The first method is to opaque the figure out on the negative, make a print, then apply some gray tones to soften the background, and spray with lacquer.

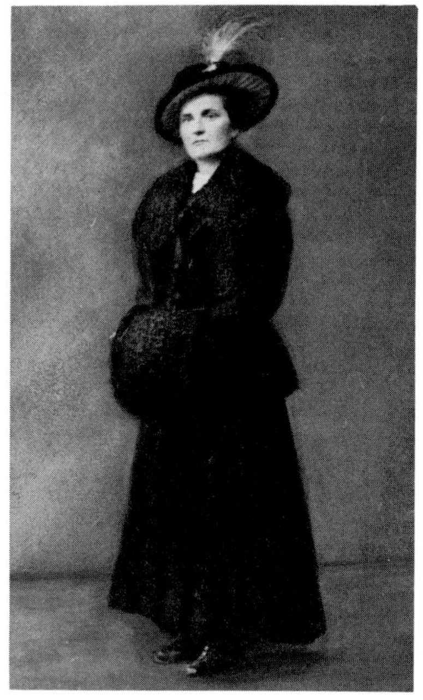

Fig. 63B. The second method is to copy the print, spray the copy print with matte lacquer, and work the figure out with monotone oil colors. The retoucher can then make a new negative of the retouched print. If it is a question of just one print, the first method is more convenient. It avoids making the second negative. However, if more pictures are desired, the second method would be preferable. (See section on Opaquing.)

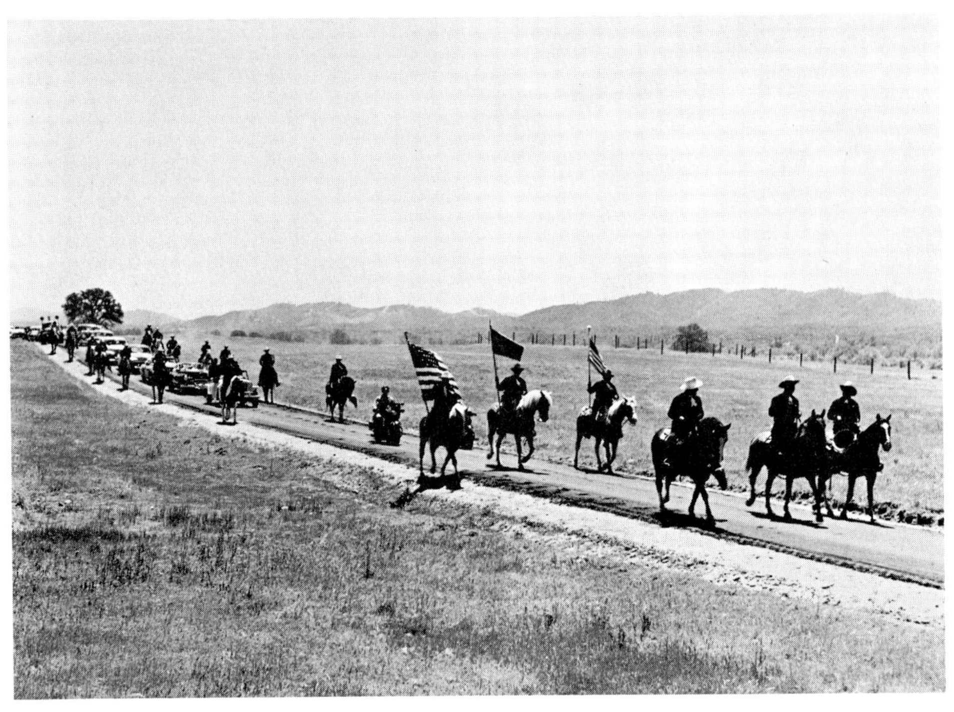

Fig. 64A. Print from original negative. Adding clouds to landscape is probably simplest technique in dye retouching.

overdoing the basic application, but will give enough tone to build up stronger lines, streaks, or cloud effects. Let it dry, make a proof, and observe what you want to improve. You may either remove the taped-on "test work" and work directly on the negative, or leave it on for making the print.

CLOUDS IN BACKGROUND

A landscape picture can be improved by strengthening cloud formation or adding clouds to a flat sky. Also, some very interesting cloud effects (similar to the expensive hand-painted studio backdrops) can be simulated on a medium-dark portrait background. In fact, one may do various light streak effects with interesting results. The technique is simple and worth trying.

Technique: Moisten the swab in water and then immerse it

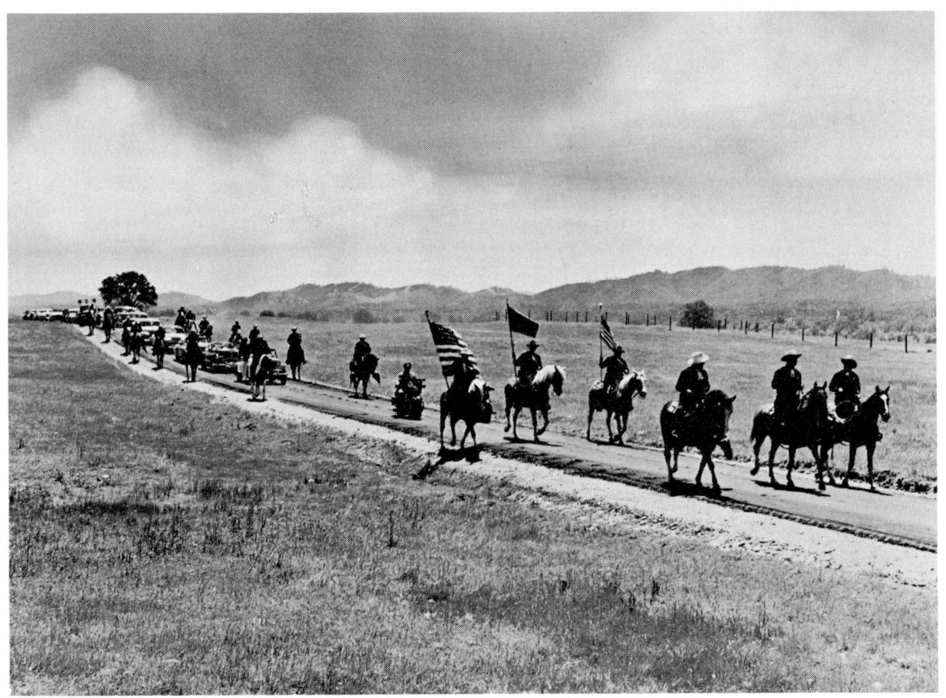

Fig. 64B. Clouds added by dye application (with swab) make picture interesting and add movement to it.

in dye. Work in *small* circular or oblong motions, keeping to the form of the cloud effect on the negative. The top of the cloud is done first to get a better separation from the sky density. With wetted cotton swab (squeezed out), dab the edges of the clouds for distant effect. A strong cloud formation should be done with straight application. Make sun proofs to determine how you like the effect. The negative must be dry before it is placed in the printing frame.

If the picture lacks clouds, one can create them in the same way as above. To get a picturesque and natural effect, apply dye in sweeping motion (across negative, back-and-forth) along the horizon line, or halfway between horizon and top of sky. The highlights of individual clouds are then strengthened as desired. (See Fig. 64.) Fixed-out film, as mentioned before, will be helpful for these experiments.

Photographers will find the ready-mixed K. West Dye invaluable. Where areas are lost in the shade, they can be brightened with a few touches of the brush or the swab, without the help of intensifier or other laborious darkroom procedures in most cases. Highlights can be added for better separation and clarity of detail, as in trees, leaves, waves on water, or other objects needing to be improved by contrast of light and shade. Only a few minutes are required to obtain such effects, through which photography gains endless scope and variety.

NOTE: The K. West Dye is excellent in retouching separation negatives or for spotting in lithography technique.

Opaquing

Opaquing (blocking out background) is necessary when a perfectly clear white background is desired. It is an important phase of commercial and portrait photography and should be mastered by every retoucher.

In portraiture and in commercial work, such as catalog outlays, photomontage, or advertising art, the demand for retouchers with a knowledge of opaquing seems to be continually increasing. A good opaquing job leaves a clear-cut outline of the subject on the negative. Opaque colors were discussed in Chapter 2. It is up to the individual to choose the method best suited to his task. One advantage of opaquing is that the application can be completely washed off without harm to the negative.

Opaquing on Portraits: Opaquing is used extensively in reproduction of photographs when a photo of one person in a group has to be printed, or when the background is objectionable. If the photographer is in possession of the negative, the work is done on the original film.

When only a print is submitted from which the person's photo has to be reproduced, a *copy negative* must be made. The unwanted parts of the negative are then covered with opaque. Besides opaquing, retouching on the face may be necessary. This has already been mentioned in a previous chapter, under "Restoring Old Prints."

Particularly on portraits, a soft edge or muted outline of the person is desirable. The retoucher having the ordinary retouching tools needs only, in addition, an opaquing color and an inexpensive brush, No. 000 or 00. (Never use your good dye-work brush for opaquing.)

Technique: Apply dope to the emulsion side of the negative, and with a dull-pointed 2B or 3B pencil, outline the head and shoulders. Go over the outline several times to make it about one-sixteenth of an inch wide. Be sure to make a proof to see if the outline is correct and the edges are not ragged. After making the first proof, turn the negative over *to the glossy side* and begin opaquing. Prepare opaque color in a small dish or bottle cap, according to instructions given with the product. Make a brush stroke test on the background to see if the color is thick enough to cover the film with one or two strokes. The color should *flow freely* from the brush and not form lumps when applied.

Then proceed to outline the figure (or whatever subject you wish to leave in the picture) to the penciled border, starting at the top of the head and working down. Once the outline around the subject is made, the rest of the background can be filled in freely with a larger brush. (See Fig. 65.)

Should the brush overlap into the area to be exposed, take a small piece of absorbent cotton, wrap it over a skewer or tooth pick, and dip it in water. Squeeze excess water out and carefully correct the outline by working *along the image.* Keep changing the cotton to avoid muddiness caused by smearing the opaque color. Since it is the glossy side of the negative that is worked upon, no damage will be caused by moistening the film.

If the pencil outline is not smooth enough or correct, one can take the etching knife and with a very careful, gentle motion of the tip, scrape the pencil border into better shape.

Carefully inspect the opaqued background for specks or thin areas where opaque did not completely cover the emulsion. Sometimes these little bare specks are noticed only after the

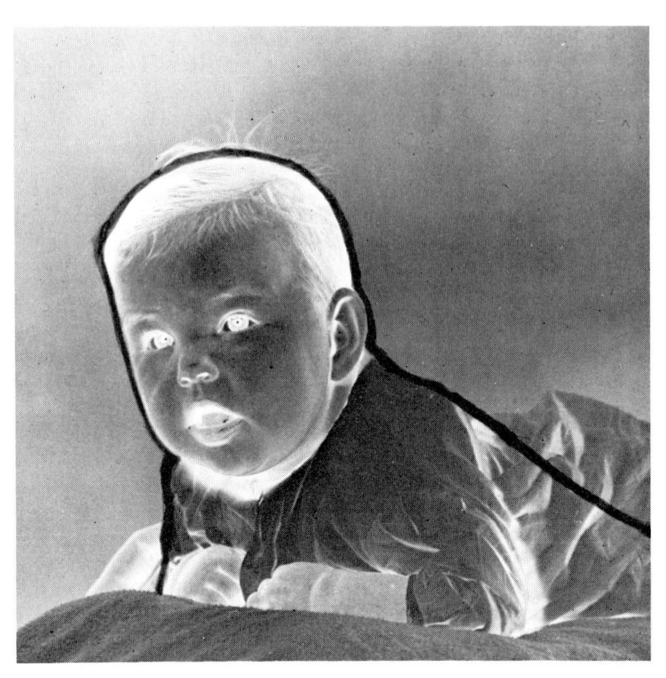

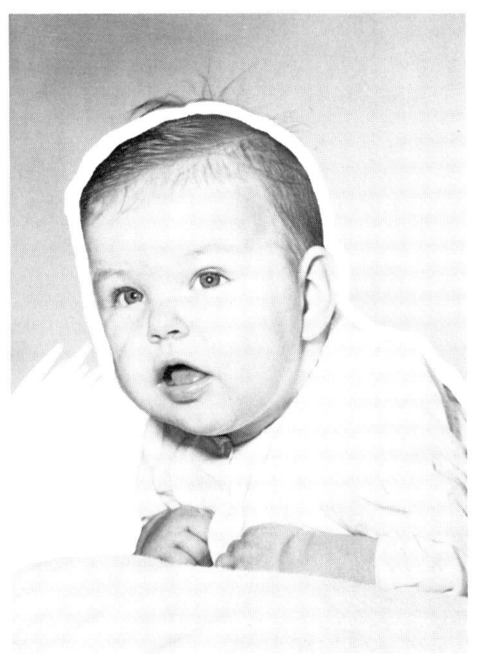

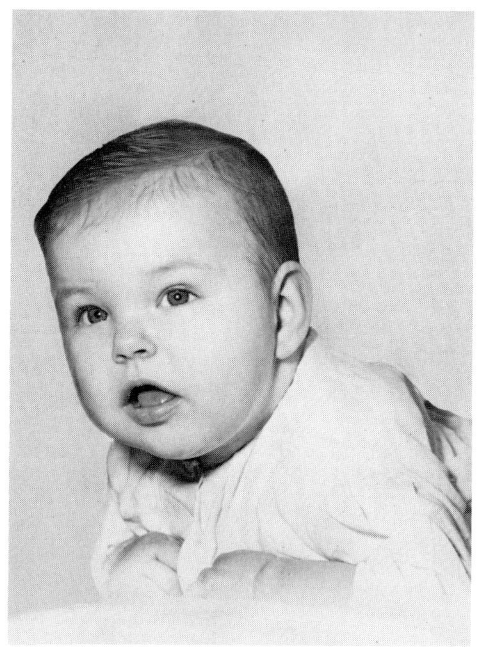

Fig. 65A (Left, top). How opaque outline looks on negative. This can be done with fine brush and liquid opaque or with very soft 2B pencil. Fig. 65B (Left, bottom). Outline and indication of fill-in brush strokes on postive proof. Fig. 65C (Above). After opaquing, graphite softened stark white background. Baby face was also retouched.

opaque color has dried. They need touching up with the brush; otherwise they will appear on the print as black spots. Let the negative dry completely before making a sun proof, or if possible have an enlarged, printed proof made for an important order.

Commercial Work: Opaquing of photographs of furniture, fixtures, machinery, or almost any advertised product is usually left to the skilled artists in the employ of advertising agencies. However, the retoucher often has a request from an independent commercial photographer who will appreciate the combined techniques of retouching and opaquing.

Tips: To opaque long straight lines, cut strips of black or red masking tape and place them directly on the glossy side wherever necessary. This procedure will save one the tedious drudgery of outlining with a ruling pen or pencil. A finely pointed china marking pencil is very convenient for outlining in portrait and commercial work. It is applied to the glossy, as opposed to the emulsion side (where the 2B pencil is used), and can easily be used to scrape into an intricate detail with the etching knife, without fear of damaging the film.

Once the outline or tape is in the proper place, you can fill in the rest with a fine brush, watching for those tiny pinholes that appear as you go along, covering the film.

To remove opaque color place the negative in a dish under running water and leave it there till all opaque is gone. Water will not remove the marks made by the china marking pencil or regular pencil. After the negative is clear of opaque, hang it up to dry in the usual manner. Then remove pencil marks with retouching medium or benzene.

NOTE: For all previously mentioned methods of negative corrections, the retoucher has now a great choice of dyes and spotting colors. They are mainly anilin dyes and more or less resemble one another. Retouch Methods Co. products are excellent, and so are Kodak or Marshall Co. brands. What the professional retoucher needs to do is experiment a little, make tests on negatives, and judge for himself what works best for him.

CHAPTER 8

Print Retouching and Spotting

The negative retoucher will doubtless always be a good finisher and spotter, for print retouching is only the reverse of negative retouching. Much depends on the presentation of a neat, spotless print. The photographer who has not taken time to give his pictures that touch of perfection has never grasped the final phase of photographic art. Again, as in any technique, it is not a question of how much time is consumed, but rather, how one simplifies the technique with best results. The retoucher who works steadily in a photo studio has a great advantage over the free-lance retoucher, who seldom has a chance to be part of the final stage of print finishing.

Frequently, a retoucher has to cope with such drastic corrections or problems of enlargements from small negative images that it is impossible to do everything on the negative. When printed without diffusion, these will frequently show a roughness of texture that needs to be lightly worked over on the print. To produce a soft effect on heavily retouched negatives the photographer should diffuse as much as the traffic allows.

The methods of working up backgrounds with water color, powdered dyes, chalks, pencils, etc., are almost nonexistent in the modern studio. Time has become an expensive, important factor, and laborious photo-finishing has become almost a lost art among spotters and finishers.

Also, the modern trend is toward less pretentious photography, where plain backgrounds and simple props are used in portraiture. Only in glamour publicity stills do we find elaborate backdrops, but work is mostly confined to movie studios, where much airbrush work is done by technicians who have devoted years solely to this particular occupation.

Airbrush technique is not mentioned in this book in conjunction with retouching techniques because airbrush technique, although in many aspects similar to retouching, involves an entirely different approach. The reader who wishes to learn this technique can find some excellent books on the market. Personal instruction is also recommended. However, we shall bypass airbrush altogether and try to explain the procedures that are closely connected to the retoucher's technique.

Our foremost concern is with retouching and spotting the common types of picture, bypassing confusing information, description, and manipulation that tend only to perplex the novice.

Discarded prints or old photographs are of help to the student in gaining experience. Some kind photographer will not mind parting with some of them, as every studio has an accumulation of extra prints.

Equipment

Only a few incidental utensils need to be added to the existing retouching outfit. They are:

1. Plywood or beaverboard, 11″ x 14″
2. Refill leads (graphites), No. 6H and an assortment of black and grey Prisma-color pencils (two or three tones of gray)
3. Palette or saucer
4. All Purpose Dye or other spotting dyes
5. Double-edged razor blade
6. Bleaching solution: Etchadine and Spott Off (optional)

Preparing for Work

Spotting should be done in daylight if at all possible. Working against the light should be avoided; it causes eyestrain and distorts proper judgment of tone quality. When spotting must be done under electric light, a blue daylight, mazda, or fluorescent tube should be used. Light should fall over the left shoulder to minimize glare.

Prepare a working area on the table with utensils at the right side. Fill the saucer with water, sharpen all pencils (including softer ones), and tape or tack the print to the board. Thumbtacks should be pushed in at the very rim so that half of the head holds the photograph and the other half of the

Fig. 66. Prints are easier to handle when tacked down. Very small spots or skin texture corrections are easier to make with hard pencil.

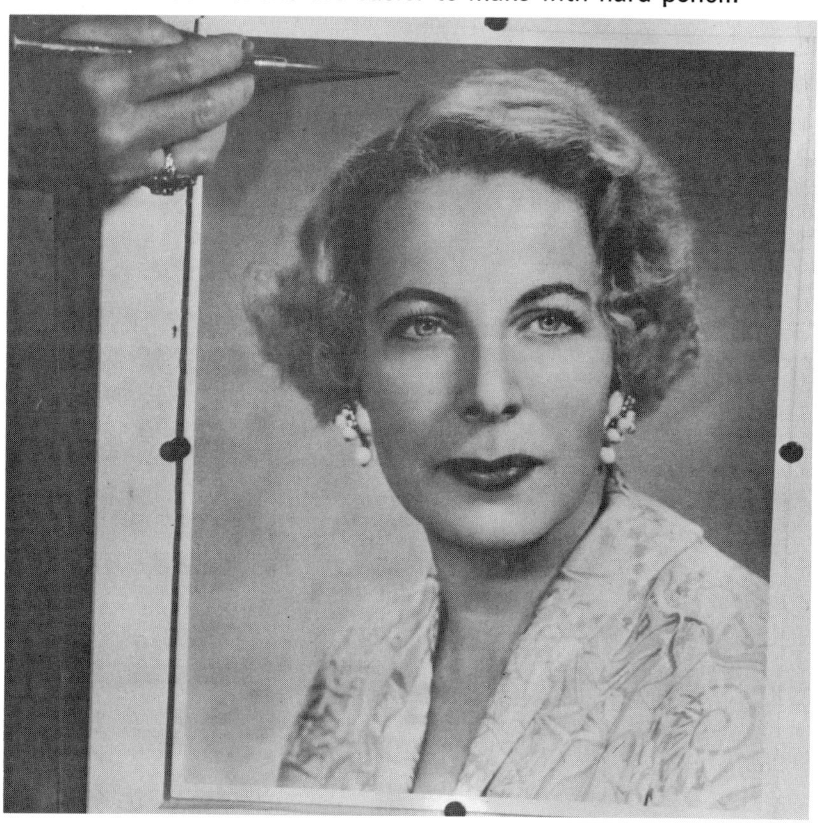

head is situated on the board (Fig. 66). Tape is not very practical, because it rips off part of the paper surface when removed. A few drops of turpentine should be rubbed over the photograph to put it in perfect condition for spotting and also to remove eventual finger marks.

Home-made Etching Knife

As mentioned above, the store-bought etcher should not be used for etching on paper. However, an additional etcher can easily be made for this purpose, from a discarded double-edged razor blade. It is a most suitable tool and can be replaced at no cost. It also has a "spring" that is most desirable in accomplishing the finest scraping on paper, reaches into the tiniest lines, and can remove the smallest speck.

To make the etcher, proceed as follows:

Hold the double-edged blade in a piece of rag or old towel. Grip it firmly between both hands and give it a slow, strong

Fig. 67A. Ordinary double-edged razor blade makes perfect etcher for print etching and saves wear on fine etching knife.

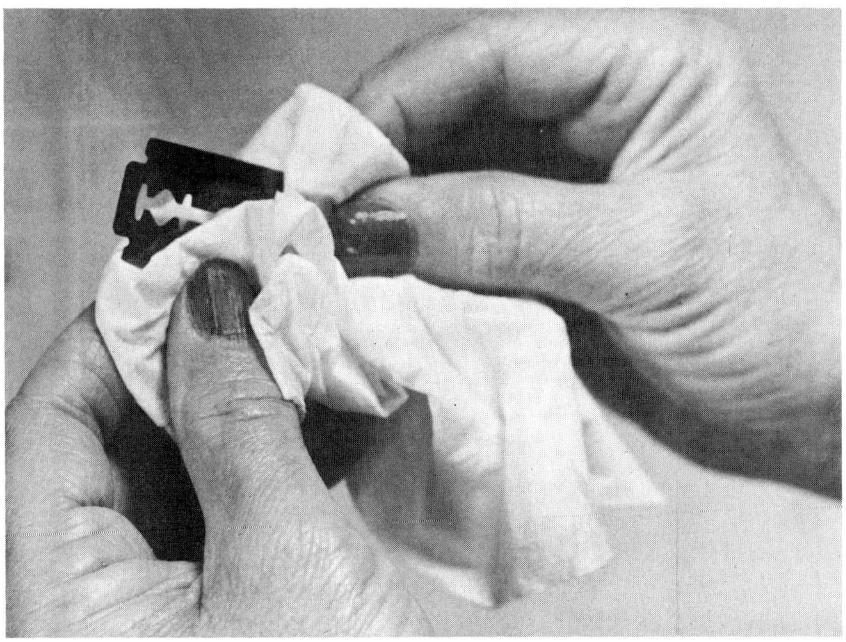

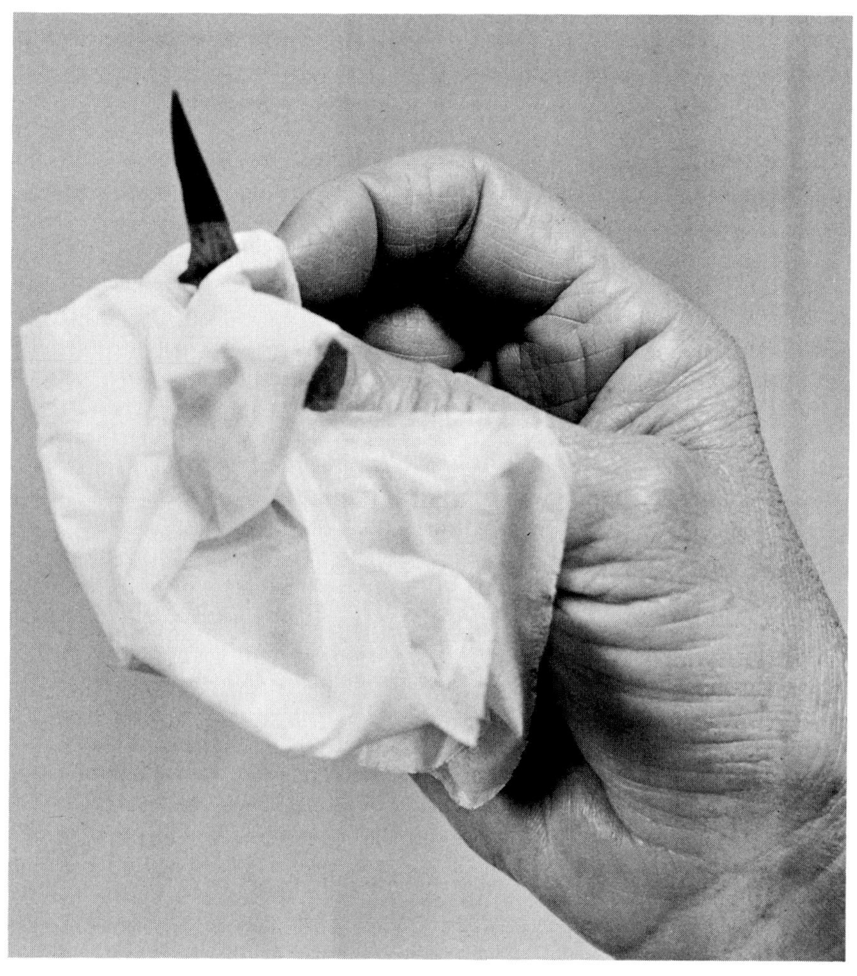

Fig. 67B. Part of razor blade suitable for etching.

twist, breaking it into two halves, lengthwise. Break one of the halves again into halves by twisting it, leaving one longer part with a rounded edge. The short end can be discarded. Make another etcher in the same way with the other half of the blade. Having thus made two slightly different etching knives, one can choose the finer blade for lines and spots, the other with a shorter edge for scraping larger areas. (See Fig. 67.)

Spotting Matte Paper

The image on the print consists of many tone values from deepest black to lightest gray. The spotting color must naturally comply in strength with the variations of these tone values. Therefore, remove spots in the darkest area first, because the brush always leaves the heaviest residue at the first touch.

It was stressed in the chapter on dye-retouching that a *moist brush* is necessary for corrections in *small areas;* in print retouching it is even more so. The paper surface absorbs the dye immediately, and removal of the dye is not as easy as on the film surface. Although a quick dab with the finger or moist cotton will take off some of the excess, caution must be exercised at all times when spotting with dye. To remedy any overdone dye-retouching on prints, put a few drops of regular ammonia in a pan with water and soak the print for a while. Once the print is dry, work can continue. One can also apply the bleaching solution locally. (See page 128.)

SPOTTING ON BLACK TONES

The K. West Dye is not a black dye and thus will not be suitable for deep gray or black tones to be spotted. For this purpose use the excellent Spotone colors, Kodak or Marshall black dyes. These dyes have to be diluted and a drop-by-drop method of application employed. The instruction sheet with each make gives an appropriate formula for different shades. When using the *opaque* colors on the disk, wet a fine spotting brush and remove some of the black color. Mix colors together on the palette and try for the right shade on the rim of the disk, twirling the brush to a fine point. Again, a glassine envelope can be used to determine the right shade. Apply the spotting color (opaque or dye) with accurate touches, hitting the very center of the exposed white speck and being careful not to overlap onto the adjoining print area. Color should be applied correctly the first time, since the second touch may remove the first layer. A loaded brush will spread the color and make it look worse than before.

If the dark tone of the print has a warm black or brownish cast (bromide prints), a speck of color dye or sepia (brown) from the disk will produce almost any shade. At first you will have to juggle the spotting colors, but soon your eyes become very aware of the right tone value, recognizing at a glance what color or how much of the dye should be mixed for a matching tone.

An excellent way to spot out tiny dust specks on very dark areas is with a black watercolor pencil (any make). Moisten the tip with saliva and apply straight to spot with a soft picking motion. The Colorama refills (mentioned later) are also excellent tools. Without moistening, the color pencils render a good cover-up on medium densities and blend very well.

NOTE: A perfect ready-mixed spotting dye for all brown-toned papers is K. West's Gold Tone Spotter. This dye is not only useful for spotting *toned papers* but also is applicable in *color spotting, color negatives,* and *color prints.*

The Gold Tone Spotter can be applied undiluted from the bottle for brown-toned paper. When dark brown areas are to be spotted, mix a few drops from the bottle with the brown *opaque color* from the disk. Wash out the brush before using it again.

SPOTTING ON MEDIUM DARK AREAS

This is where the ready-mixed K. West Dye is at its unsurpassed best. Without mixing or testing one can spot out specks with a few quick touches, or enhance certain parts of the face or clothing. The dye-retouching cannot be detected even by holding the print obliquely to the light.

Eyelashes look more natural when a few strokes are added to them or a fine line is drawn along the eyelids, giving depth to the eye.

Pupils can be spotted for better expression. Using the dye alone, without the black spotting color, will prevent a beadlike effect.

Eyebrows can be shaped, thickened, or evened out with short stippling strokes, conforming to the pattern of hair growth.

Lips are easily corrected, shaped, or strengthened. Strong highlights on lower lips can be subdued.

Shadows on neck can be filled in in part. On older people a few touches along the jawline give it a better shape.

Hairdos should be filled in loosely with brush strokes to eliminate gaps. For lighter color, the All Purpose Dye or other spotting colors are fine. For small areas, the black colorama or other black pencil, either moistened or dry, will do the job.

Details of clothes and shadows on folds can be accentuated with a slightly loaded brush or swab, using rather quick motions.

Two important things to remember when working with dye:

1. Use quick motions with brush or swab for larger areas.

2. Use slow and deliberate strokes when working on small space or minute detail. Brush should be almost dry.

SPOTTING LIGHT TONES ON FACE AND BACKGROUND

Dilute a few drops of dye with a few drops of water in a bottle cap or saucer, or on the palette. Use a minimum of dye, just enough to keep the tip of the brush from splitting.

For retouching skin texture, where tiny cracks or spots from uneven negative-retouching appear, there is nothing better than the *regular retouching lead.* A hard pencil, 5H, 6H, or even 7H, will perfectly match the lightest tone on face or background. The fine pencil point will penetrate beautifully into the paper surface with such accuracy that a beginner can undoubtedly accomplish better and faster work with pencils than by unskilled brush retouching. The pencil stroke, conforming to the grain of the paper in vibrating, poking, or quivering touches, is practically the same as that used in negative retouching. In fact, many well-known photographers will resort to the old art of fine pencil retouching for character portraiture or pictorial photographs.

A light rubbing with a clean index finger over the applied pencil work will make it adhere to the print better and will leave no trace of strokes. Pencil retouching will not rub off, contrary to the general assumption. If soft pencils have been used, or if for some reason the pencil marks show, one can always spray the print with a matte spray (*e.g.*, Marshall's Pre-Color Spray) for an even surface.

A few drops of turpentine on a tissue paper will remove all pencil work from the print, and leave it spotlessly clean.

NOTE: For larger area, apply dye in diluted form with a swab. Moisten the area locally with a small sponge or cotton swab, applying the dye in loose, even motions. Any surplus should be dabbed off as the work proceeds. This technique is called giving a "wash of color," since it resembles watercolor work. For corrections of uneven densities, particularly along edges, which are very difficult to blend in tone, again the various grades of retouching leads will be most appropriate for blending.

USING THE ETCHER

It is not recommended to use the etcher extensively on any print surface. Dark spots should be taken care of in negative-retouching, but if dark spots appear on background or face in spite of retouching, a delicate scraping will remove the spots. With the fingernail one can smooth the surface down and apply *pencil* to get the exact tone. Sometimes a dark hair can be nicely etched out. Etching (with a razor tip) is also a good way to make catchlights in the eye appear strong without using the white opaque color. If much etching has been performed on the print one can spray again with Marshall's Pre-Color Spray or a glossy spray. Sprays of several makes are available in photo supply and art supply stores. Follow instructions on labels.

The print should not be handled while it is drying, as fingerprints and dust specks will show up on the varnished picture.

A black-and-white print or sepia-toned paper that is being used for oil coloring or tinting *should not be etched beforehand.* The oil colors settle into the exposed surface and make it more difficult to correct. All spotting of such prints should be left *until oil coloring is finished* and the print is dry.

BLEACHING

Another way to brighten dark areas on prints is to use bleach. There are several ready-made products on the market. Among others, Spot Off is effective when instructions are carefully followed. It is a controllable dark spot remover as well as a general reducer to lighten dark tones on prints. It will take the densest black down to a pure white in a matter of seconds, and it can be modified to reduce any print tone just slightly. (This is good to use when too-heavy dye-retouching has been applied and one wants to reduce it locally without washing the entire print.)

Spot Off is suitable for removing black specks, cleaning up whites of eyes, teeth, etc. Spot Off (or another bleach sold for photography) works on all types of papers from matte to glossy. Being colorless, it will not stain the print and its work is invisible. It is sold in two bottles: the "B" is the Bleacher and "A" is the Accelerator. The more "A" solution that is added to the "B," the faster it works. As in all photo experimentation, never make your first attempt on a photograph meant for the customer. Try one or two methods to determine which will work best. Highly recommended products for various spotting and bleaching purposes are manufactured by Jamieson Products Co., 9341 Peninsula Drive, Dallas, Texas 75218. They will mail price list and information sheets on all their products upon request.

Many print finishers favor a ten per cent Clorox solution. To make stock use one drop of Clorox to ten drops of distilled water. The solution is applied with the tip of the brush for small areas and with a swab when bigger areas have to be subdued. As the tone is fading out, a small wad of cotton saturated with water should be dabbed over the particular area in order to stop the bleaching action. Blot off the surplus water and let it dry. Wetting larger parts of the print is better done on the back of a metal tray near a sink, where working with water will not be inconvenient.

Spotting Semi-Matte Paper

Dye instructions applying to matte prints are to be followed for semi-matte paper too. If a print is made for reproduction purposes, a glossy or semi-glossy paper is generally used. Retouching with dye can then be bolder in execution and thus give a better contrast for the final print. When a duplicate negative is made, a great deal of tonal quality can be added to an otherwise faded or flat picture, as I mentioned in the section on "Reproductions of Old Photographs."

Background "washes" can also be applied directly to the semi-matte print, which seems ideally suited for dye retouching. They blend into the paper surface without a trace, leaving no dull spots to give away the correction.

If a copy negative is being made from the semi-glossy print, the exact matching color of dye is not of great importance. It will reproduce in gray tones only, and any additional retouching can be taken care of on the copy negative.

Prints for display purposes, such as publicity portraits, will be under critical observation. The spotting must exactly match the local shade. Either reduce the dye with a few drops of water to a very light shade or add a speck of black color from the spotting disk to the dye for darker tones. Make a test for the right shade on the palette before touching the print.

Some texture corrections can be made with soft pencils. If they don't "take," then it is best to spray the print with any dull lacquer (McDonald, Marshall, etc.). Then apply the graphite or even the previously mentioned spotting pencil over the area. Spray the print again with either matte or glossy lacquer, as the need may be. (Since there is a great selection of spraying lacquers now on the market, every spotter or retoucher should have at least two different lacquers on hand. They are also needed for all color print spotting, which is explained in Part II.) An application of retouching medium over the part to be spotted will render a good base for pencil strokes. It will not dull the sheen of the paper surface, and the most intricate spotting can be achieved without detection.

Using a Clorox solution or another bleaching agent is preferable to etching with a knife or razor blade. The knife scrapes the sheen to such an extent that corrective work is always obvious when closely inspected. (See "Bleaching," page 128.) To restore gloss to a print, use Marshall's glossy fixative Spray-Glass or the non-glossy Pro-Tek-To Spray.

Spotting a Glossy Print

The slick surface of glossy paper most closely resembles the shiny surface of the film negative, and thus dye-retouching will prove to be the simplest and most suitable spotting method. Finishing glossy prints seems to be the most dreaded task for a photographer, as almost any type of spotting color leaves a dull and obviously corrected mark. It will be gratifying for the photo-finisher to use the ready-mixed K. West Dye and see it disappear into the shiny surface without leaving a trace.

Glossy prints are much sharper and usually have a stronger tone-contrast than other printing papers. They are used mainly for newspaper, fashion, commercial, and many other reproduction purposes. If the dark areas are pure black, it is advisable to use Spotone, Kodak or Marshall spotting dyes, slightly diluted if necessary.

Procedure on medium and light densities is the same as that described for other photographic paper surfaces. When dye is applied to larger areas with the *cotton swab,* the wetted paper may lose its sheen. If this occurs, one may apply regular retouching medium and rub it over the entire print. Also, spraying with the Spray-Glass varnish will restore gloss.

For correction of overdone dye-work, wash the print under the faucet. Observe to what degree the dye is fading in strength as the washing proceeds, and when the desired tone is reached place the print on a squeegee plate, face downward. Remove excess air bubbles or moisture between the print and plate by passing a squeegee roller over the back of the print or wiping it off with a clean cloth. The entire surface of the print should be in contact with the plate. When dry, the print will "pop" off and its high gloss will be restored.

To remove dye entirely, soak the print in water to which a few drops of ammonia have been added. After the dye is completely washed out place the print on a squeegee plate and proceed as before.

With these corrective methods at one's disposal there is no reason why trying out different effects should not be interesting and exciting to anyone making photography his livelihood or hobby. The retoucher may develop some variations on techniques as he gains experience. For the beginner the possibility of spoiling a print or a negative is nonexistent as long as tested procedures mentioned here are followed.

Bleaching of spots has been previously described.

Etching glossy prints is out of the question, because the surface gelatin layer is destroyed by scraping with the blade. Sometimes spotting over a dark spot may be greatly minimized by applying a touch of white pencil or using the white opaque color from the spotting disk.

Once the fundamentals of print spotting (that pencils and dyes may be employed in combination or separately) are understood, the print surface or tone will make little difference. The general technique seldom varies.

CHAPTER 9

Graphite Powder and Monochrome Techniques

Graphite Technique (For Matte Papers Only)

Print retouching could not be dealt with completely without the inclusion of a chapter on graphite technique, which resembles airbrush or watercolor work. It is particularly appropriate when opaquing of negatives has produced a stark white background, when the contrast of dark and light parts needs an intermediate shade, or when a light tone has to be accentuated by deeper contrast.

This effective method of workmanship is often overlooked by photo-finishers, who consider it a time-consuming and elaborate procedure. Its great merit can really be appreciated when comparison is made between a print that has been treated with graphite and one that has not. The short time it takes to accomplish a beautiful and artistic effect should induce anyone to experiment with graphite powder on a matte paper at the earliest opportunity.

Working with graphite powder will not interfere with the dye method, as each in its own way fills a certain function. Although the application of dye with a brush is preferred for accentuating parts of the face or details of objects, the graphite powder should be used where shades of gray should blend into bigger areas. Once the negative and finishing techniques are combined in an intelligent adaptation, a photographer has an enormous scope of picture modification and negative improvement at his command.

It should be remembered that *all dye work must be done before graphite work.*

A good working space should be provided on the table and all utensils necessary for this work should be at arm's reach. Soft grading and tonal quality are important aspects of this technique, and are more easily observed when working in daylight.

Equipment

Spirits of Turpentine	Absorbent Cotton
Graphite Powder	Art Eraser (pearl
Swabs	eraser or rubber)

Preparing for Work

Clean the print with turpentine, since the slightest finger mark will show up when graphite dust is applied. Rub over the entire picture with a circular motion; rub it dry with cleansing tissue. Fasten the print to the board (as for spotting) and lay it aside to protect it from graphite powder.

Sprinkle a little graphite powder (dust from the container that is used for sharpening pencils) onto a folded piece of wax paper. This is also an excellent material for working with oil colors. Wax paper does not absorb the oil of the paints nor the turpentine which is mixed with the graphite dust. If a more intense gray is needed, sharpen the HB or B graphite and use it. For very light grey tones, the harder pencils are suitable.

Procedure

Make a tight wad of cotton and pick up some of the powder. Rub the cotton firmly against the wax paper, crushing the grain to an even tint. Place the print flat on the table before you. Starting at the outer corner of the background, work in deft circular motions toward the subject, very much in the same manner as when applying medium to a negative.

As the graphite is gradually absorbed by the paper surface, lighter gradations can be worked off or more powder added for deeper shades. Where the application overlaps onto the portrait, the contrast can be strengthened by erasing along the hairline, face and shoulders with a rubber eraser. If a blended tone is desired, only the highlights in certain areas should be picked up with the gum eraser.

To produce a graphite "wash" similar to airbrush, take another wad of cotton and put a couple of drops of turpentine on it. Rub in rather quick rotary motions over the background, pressing firmly and evenly as you go. A smeared effect should *not* cause concern. Through rubbing down the streaky edges, a perfectly smooth tone resembling an airbrush effect will appear. Smoothing down should be done rapidly, as the turpentine dries quickly under the touch. A few more drops added to the cotton wad will keep it in workable condition. This method is inconspicuous and ideal where a simple gray background effect is desired.

Additional shades, streaks of light, or cross-hatch effects can be produced on the basic tone with the art eraser, depending on the requirements of the portrait or subjects.

The fact that unsatisfactory work can be entirely removed with turpentine and that a print can be worked over many times till the desired effect is reached should induce some experimenting.

By using the graphite and gum technique, a background of clouds can be similarly worked up (Fig. 68). First, a light shade of gray is given to the background (or sky, in a landscape picture) with the graphite and turpentine. A tiny amount of graphite on a swab will give details of clouds and deeper patches. Highlights and contours are produced by erasing with the art gum. The eraser should be cut to a wedge shape to allow for broad highlights and the delineation of fine edges and forms.

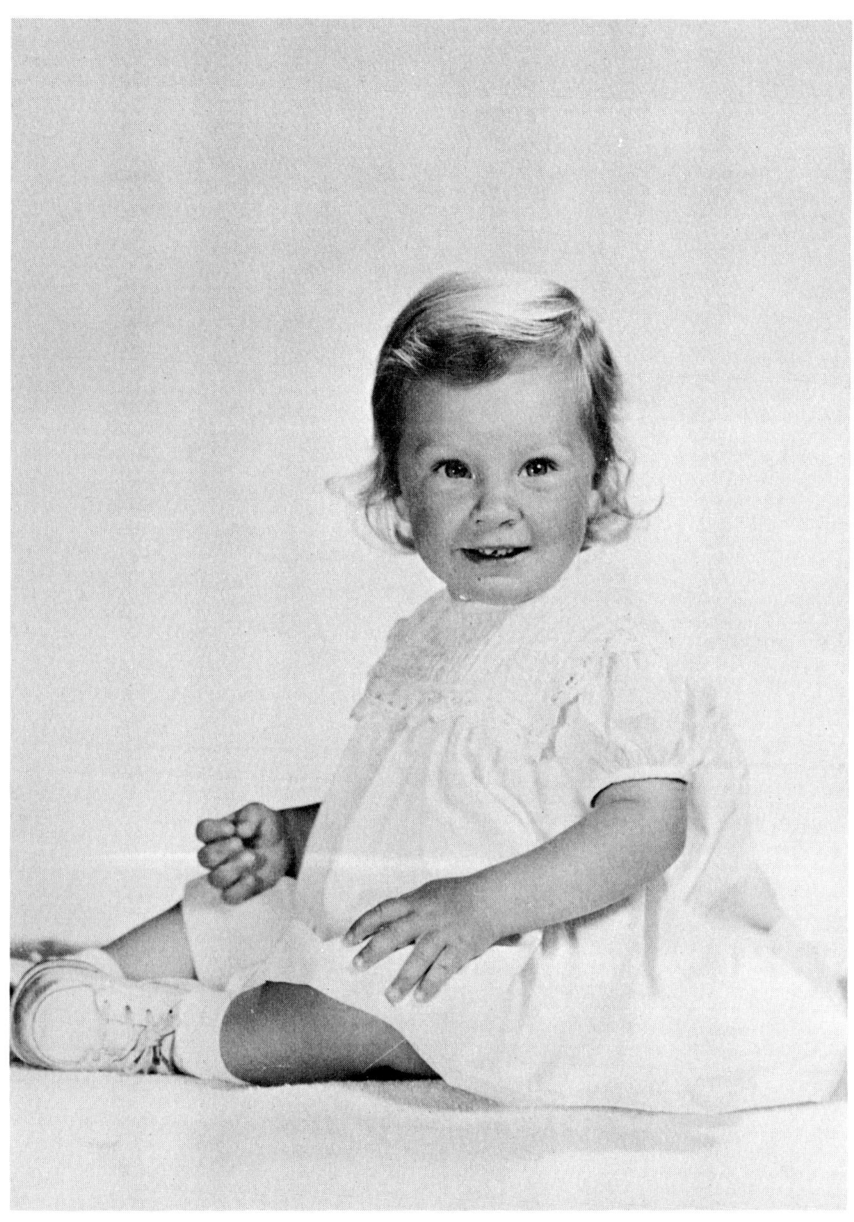

Fig. 68A. Original picture of baby. Plain background with hardly any contrast.

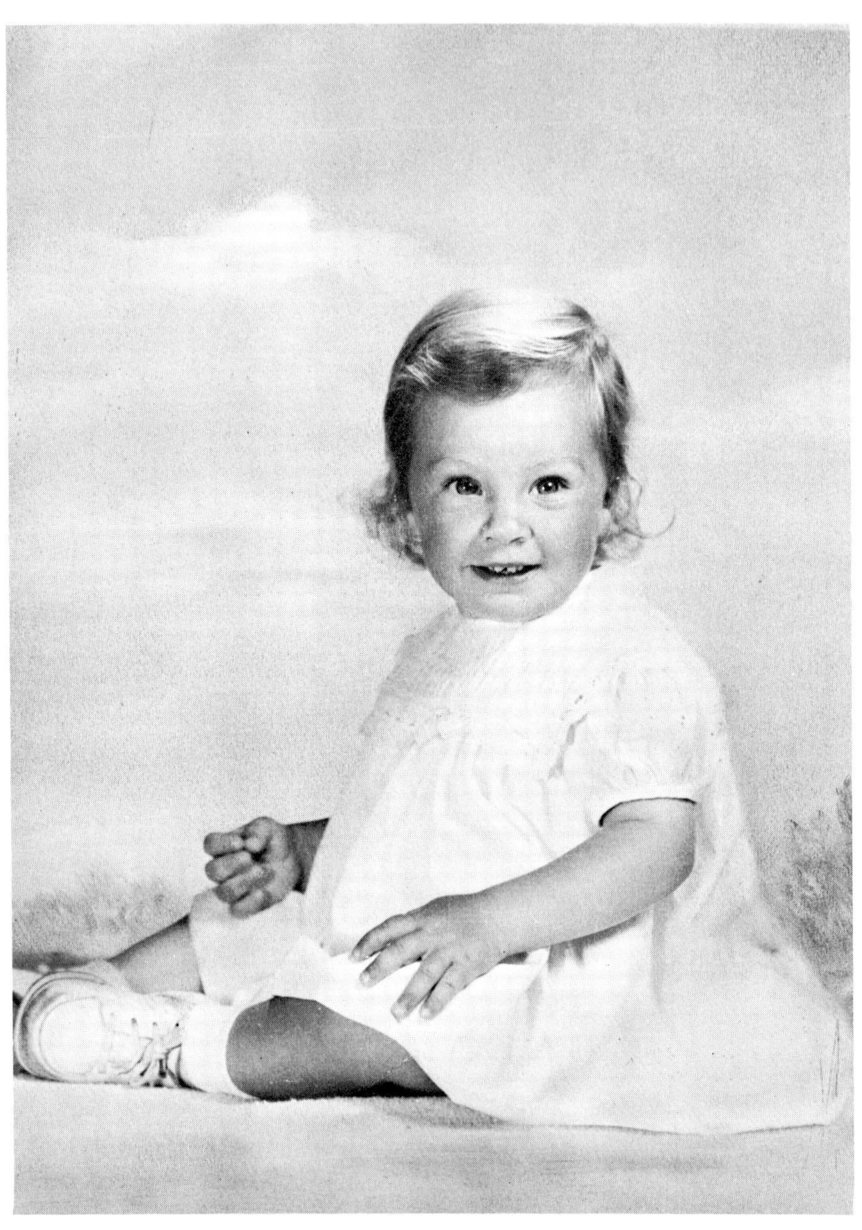

Fig. 68B. Interesting effects can be achieved by graphite or oil application. (Technique is explained in Chapter 9.) This "art" work is particularly attention-getting in displays in studio windows because it provides a welcome change from run-of-the-mill children's portraiture. Work is speedy and lucrative.

Always use dry cotton or cleansing tissue to clean off eraser grains or surplus powder from prints. Don't wipe with your fingers! The moisture on fingertips smears and mars the paper.

Parts that are too shiny on the hair, face, or clothing can be softened by the swab application. Care should be taken that the cotton holds only a little graphite at a time. Before each application, rub it on a clean piece of paper, or better yet, roll the swab over paper to obtain a clean tone. For a mere shade apply another piece of clean cotton or cleansing tissue. Highlights are produced as desired by erasing.

To protect a print that has been treated with graphite, a fixative, sold in all art supply stores, should be sprayed on. This not only permits safe handling of the photograph, but also imparts a crisper tone effect to it. Of course, the previously mentioned lacquers are also suitable for print protection.

Monochrome Technique

The treatment in monochrome (one tone) has been used by photo-artists who can demand high prices for their art work. However, the method is so simple that anyone not even familiar with painting or transparent photo oil coloring can master it after a few experiments. Particularly in photo-copy work, giving background to opaqued prints, and the like, the method about to be described will elevate an unpretentious print to a work of art.

This technique achieves changes on the print without the help of any color except the tone of the print itself. In other words, it can be applied to black-and-white or any toned photograph, *after* the print is finished.

It is to be regretted that the tempo of our times is such that this technique has been practically discarded as being too time-consuming. Perhaps it has never been properly explained to students in photography schools, where more and more attention is being paid to the scientific methods of photography.

Yet, the monochrome technique is the quickest and best money-saving procedure for the photographer who will take the time to utilize it in every way he can. In fact, the oil color

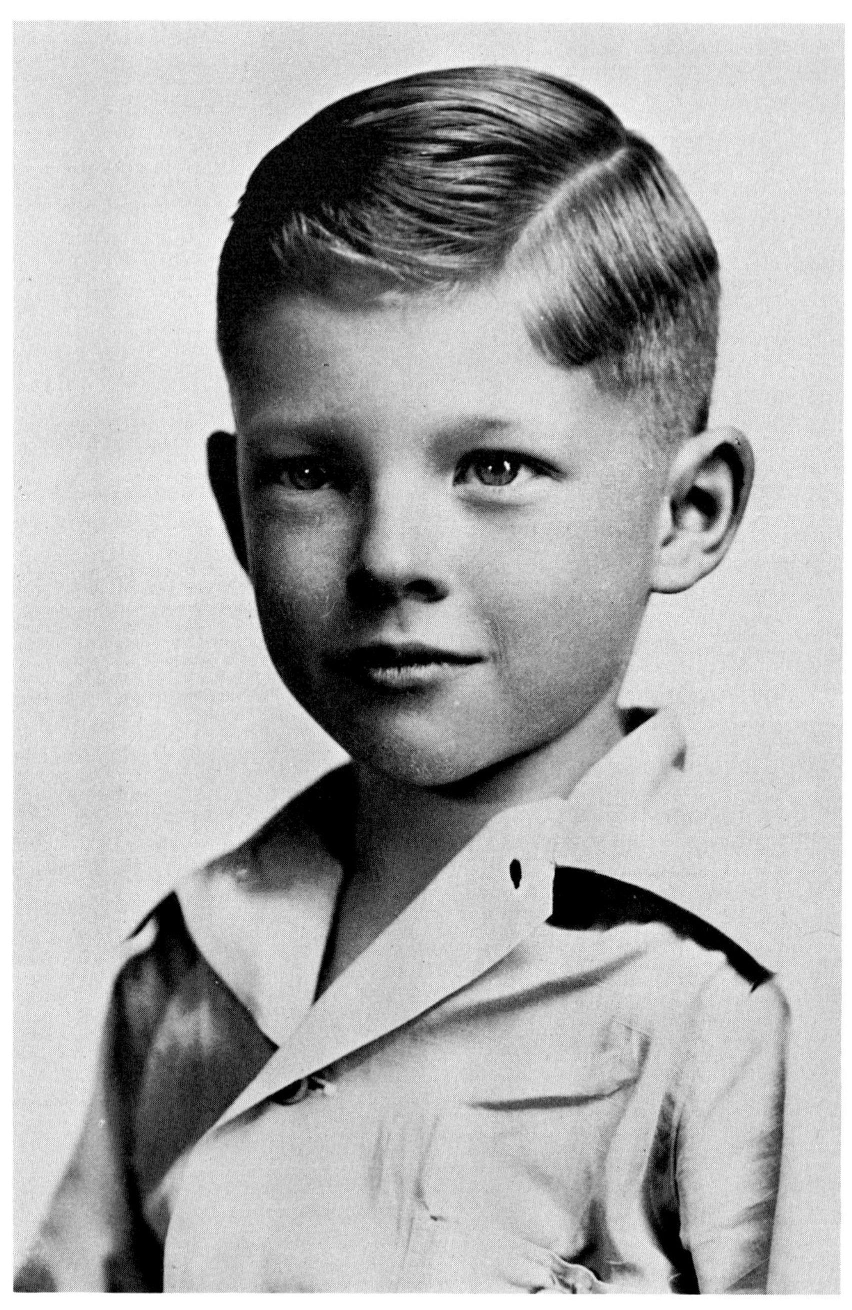

Fig. 69A. Another example of picture that needs stronger background. This print is in sepia tone.

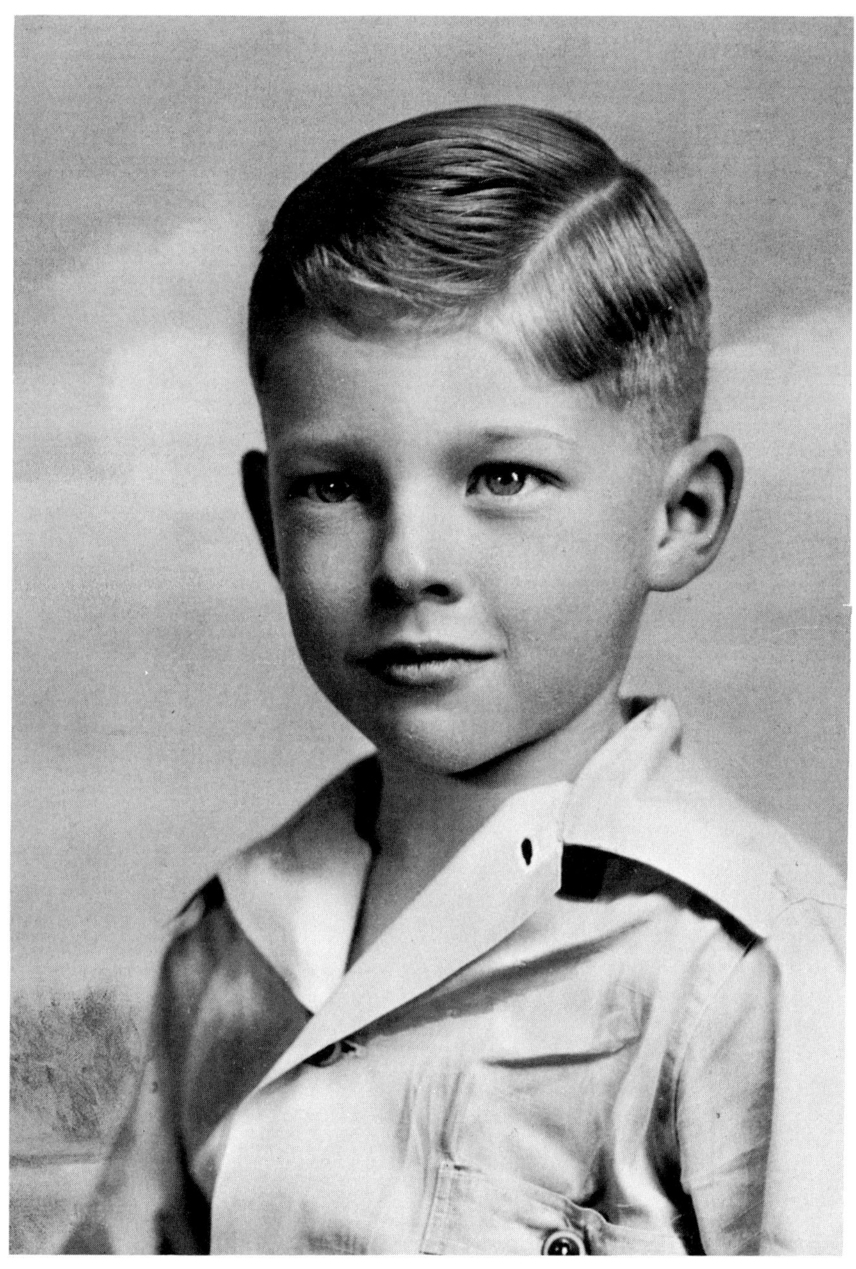

Fig. 69B. For brown-toned paper, Verona Brown, Sepia, or Raw Umber oil colors must be mixed for matching tone.

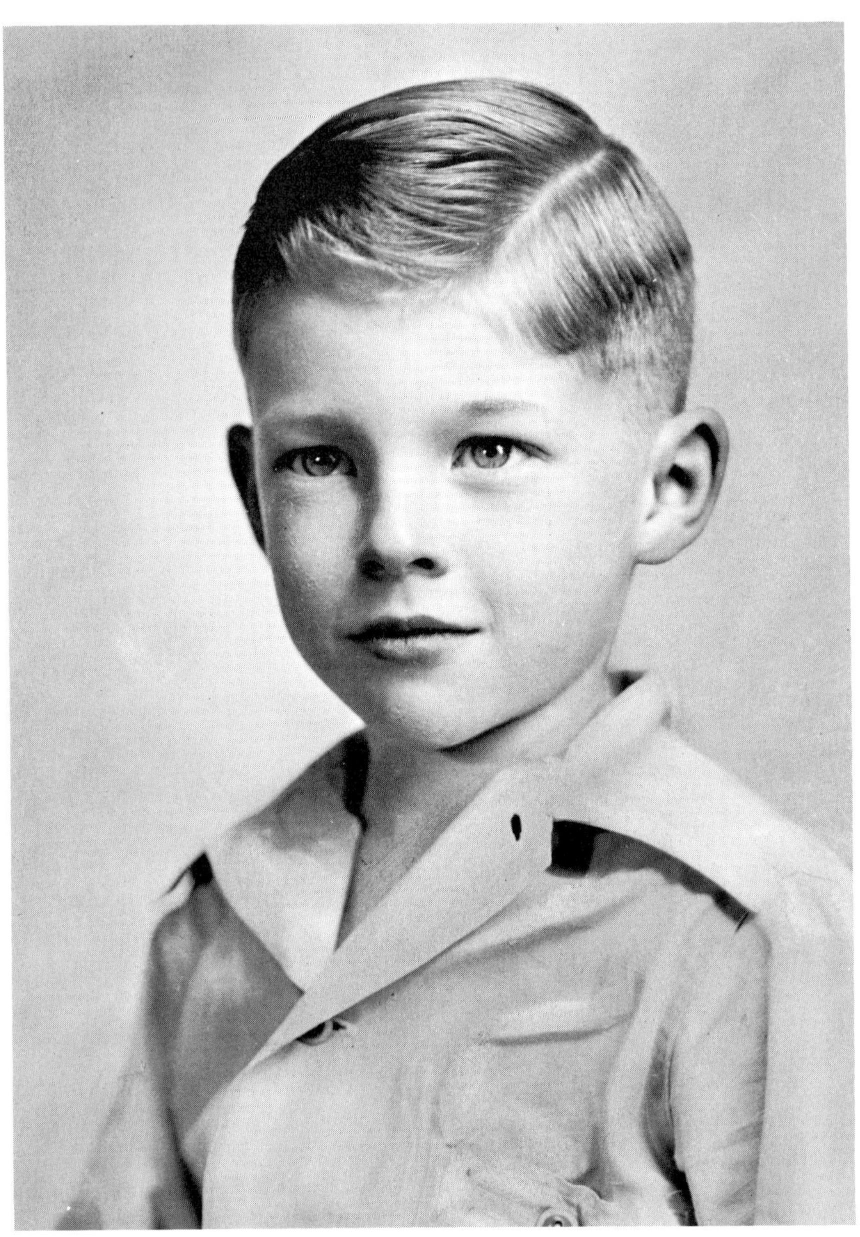

Fig. 69C. Background may be kept simple, or given effect of expensive backdrop. Technique (monochrome) is fully described in *Hand Coloring Your Photographs with Oils and Dyes* (Amphoto). Scenery and bushes were done with gentle dabs, using tuft of cotton.

method of changing backgrounds or adding effects of light and shadow to a print may in many instances be preferable to the graphite method, which requires a rather swift working of the powder.

Figures 69B and C were executed in oil color (monochrome) technique, and one can readily see the possibilities in the visual effect by comparing one with the other.

Equipment

Marshall's Neutral Tint and black oil colors
Marshall's Zinc White or Titanium White
Tube of Extender, brush, swab and turpentine, and cotton (for black-and-white)
Marshall's Sepia and Verona Brown oil colors (for brown-toned papers)

Procedure

If the photograph to be worked on is in black-and-white, use Neutral Tint with some black to match the print accurately. Apply the color with a little Extender on a small tuft of cotton to the parts of the photograph you wish to change. If an object or an entire background has to be blocked out (restoration of old photographs), mix it with white, which will make the tone opaque.

Next the background has to be gone over with a flat sable brush, No. 2 or No. 4, and blended down evenly. For a transparent gray hue, the cotton application will be sufficient. With a clean tuft of cotton, one may rub down areas that have to be lightened. Add black if a darker tone is necessary.

The more Extender one adds to the color, the thinner it becomes. Extender or turpentine will also clean off paint or pick up detail to purify the white of the print. Of help to the reader who wishes to go further into the aspect of oil coloring techniques on prints, my book *Hand Coloring Your Photographs with Oil and Dyes* (Amphoto, $2.50) is recommended. The above-mentioned techniques are only briefly touched upon, as they should already be a part of the retoucher's art.

In the section on "Restoring Old Photographs," page 110, we talked about the use of dyes and pencils. However, the graphite or oil coloring techniques can be a part of the previous procedures.

Monochrome work on *toned paper* requires the use of the brown range of colors. In addition to Sepia, Verona Brown, Raw Umber, and Burnt Umber will definitely match any brown-toned paper. Mixing one or two of these colors together may give the exact tone of the paper. Sometimes white can be added for an opaque background, just as, we previously noted, black or Neutral Tint will produce gray tones. Turpentine is used for cleaning the picture completely. Extender, which is softer and comes in tube form, is excellent for cleaning a background where color has overlapped onto a face or dress. It is also good when a small part of the picture has to be cleaned out. It is best applied with a cotton-tipped skewer or orange stick. A certain amount of practice is necessary in order to know how to wrap the point of the skewer and build it up from a sliver of cotton to a good-sized ball. (Refer back to Fig. 14.)

Before you begin the oil coloring of color prints you might first use the monotone technique on some photograph with a blank, uninteresting background and see what fun it is to add a dash of art to it.

PART II

Color

CHAPTER 10

Retouching Color Negatives

Little has been written to clarify the field of color retouching. From the hazy information the retoucher was able to obtain in the past he assumed that color retouching was a technique closely guarded by a few photographers and retouchers. This was the case some years ago, when color photography was limited to exclusive studios and was not as widely used as it is today.

The retoucher who knows black-and-white retouching will not find retouching of color negatives difficult. There are visual differences to consider, but the technique of using pencil and dye closely resembles previously acquired skills. However, one can use color dyes and color pencils in addition.

The following aspects of color retouching are rather hard on the retoucher:

1. The small size of film often used (roll film) requires a delicate touch with softer pencils than those used on black-and-white negatives. The slick film surface does not accept as much pencil and thus an area must be covered accurately and quickly.

2. If a film surface has been lacquered, it is necessary to remove the lacquer. This will be explained later.

3. Retouching of color negatives strains the eyes more than any other retouching work, and thus I find it the greatest drawback for the retoucher. Furthermore, the work does not pay better than regular retouching because retouching is kept to a minimum. Modeling or detailed retouching is not necessary because the color image compensates for the harsher densities of black-and-white negatives.

4. Etching cannot be attempted. Color film consists of three color layers, which get damaged by scraping. Not even the use of the abrading needle is recommended for removing spots. That which normally would be etched on a black-and-white negative must be darkened on the print with color pencils or dyes.

5. Bleaching on color negatives should not be attempted as it has never proved successful. In the future there may be a product for this purpose, but at present the process of color reduction by various methods is confined to the color laboratories.

6. Handling of color negatives must be done with the utmost care. The film, having less emulsion and being softer than black-and-white negatives, will show the smallest scratch or finger mark on the print. Anyone having the slightest tendency to sweaty or oily skin should wear cotton gloves (photographic supply stores sell them) and keep the film in its glassine envelope as much as possible.

The most confusing and at times frustrating aspect of color retouching is caused by the variety of color film now being used in photography. This means that the retoucher must apply a slightly different technique to each type of film he works with. It is imperative to have a color proof on hand in order to study the skin tone as well as the color of shadows, blemishes, or lines. The whole *trick of color negative* retouching, regardless of what color pencil or graphites are being used or what type of film is worked on, lies in the simple fact that *the retoucher puts in the color that is already on the print before him.* As an example, the shadow from eyeglasses under the eyes tend toward bluish tones; the pencils or color pencils or dyes you use *must* also produce bluish tones. Observe the color negative; it has a faint yellowish coloration, which means that *blue* tone *is* the complementary color to yellow on the negative. Freckles are reproduced as a brownish hue on the proof and can be softened with a brown pencil or brownish dye (Gold Tone Spotter is good for that). When a blemish appears red (greenish on the negative), a red pencil should be used. Once the retoucher has this simple rule of color retouching established in his mind, everything else will be easier. Addition of dyes or regular graphites of any softness are then applied over the color pencils until the retouched area conforms in tone to the surrounding tone or density. Lines on color negatives do not need heavy retouching or careful modeling as do black-and-white negatives. The color compensates for the various hues of flesh tones. However, no matter how little retouching is done on the color negatives, your touch must be extremely light. For this reason, select soft or regular graphites depending on the type of film being worked on. Keep in mind, the slicker roll films need the HB, B, and even softer pencils; sheet film (the retoucher's joy) can be worked nicely with the H and harder pencils.

At this time when so many color printing methods are being used, the studio or lab should give the retoucher a chance to make a few tests to determine which method is best suited for each type of film and printing technique. This is particularly helpful in school photography (the main source of income for the color negative retoucher) where negatives are mailed out to various retouchers in far away places. Photographers should send several test negatives with proofs on which the retoucher can jot down the dyes or pencils he used. When the print tests are made, the retoucher can readily refer to the samples and select the best technique. A retoucher who never has a chance to make tests or see his finished work will never know *why* or *how* he made a mistake. This procedure could avoid endless hours of spotting, lab rejects, and mounting costs of processing.

With the use of smaller and slicker films, which are certainly more economical and practical for machine processing, the retoucher, unfortunately, has less and less space for doing fine corrections.

However, we all have a lot to learn yet, and hopefully new types of film or processing will make it easier for all concerned to keep up with the ever expanding trends in color photography.

Informative brochures are published from time to time, and most retouching products come with descriptive directions. The Eastman Kodak Company, Rochester, New York, has good pamphlets on color retouching. Write to the above address and ask for Kodak pamphlet No. E-71, "Retouching Color Negatives," and pamphlet No. E-70, "Retouching Ektacolor Prints." Although these give information only on Kodak's own products, the retoucher can avail himself of other very good color retouching and spotting dyes now available from Retouch Methods Co., Marshall Co., or the National Retouchers Guild. The latter dyes are ready to use and simplify laborious testing of the most important hues.

Reading a Color Negative

Color Plate 1 was purposely taken to demonstrate the primary faults of a color negative that needs retouching, and also for the combination of colors of the dress, which clearly show the composite of yellow, blue-green, and red. Study this example carefully and you will learn how to read a color negative.

This picture was taken on 4″ x 5″ sheet film, and is ideal head size for overall retouching of skin defects.

1. The negative density of the face indicates a bluish-violet tone (light skin tone reproduces like this), so the new "K" dye No. I was used for the forehead, along the nose, under the eyes slightly, and in the depression on the side of the chin. The shadow on the neck tends toward brown and blue tones in the fleshy folds, and was retouched with Gold Tone Spotter. Also, the scar and freckles on the hand were softened the same way. After having applied the dyes, the negative was doped on both sides.

2. Stray hairs in background were removed with an HB pencil. Bluish veins on the hand were softened with the same graphite.

3. Red and brown colorama pencil were applied to the face, neck, and hands for finer texture retouching until the negative appeared smooth, as in illustration No. 3, the harder graphite H2 was used where necessary. The final print (No. 4) was touched up with Ideal Flesh I on the tiny highlight under left eyebrow, over one of the raised veins on the hand, and finally on the strong lip highlight. Specks on background were spotted with All Purpose Dye.

From this example, the reader can well see that he has to use every means at his command, that is, a variety of dyes, color pencils, and graphites to do the job right.

It all sounds very complicated and confusing to the novice, but it is astounding how quickly one acquires the feel for color negative retouching once the principal rules of the technique are understood. There really is not *one* definite formula, one dye, or one pencil that will magically perform all corrections. Rather, it is a combination of common sense in judging which methods will work best, and then patience and determination to master the craft. Color photography is here to stay no matter how we old-timers bemoan the easy way we could retouch black-and-white negatives and get predictable results. We are all rather new at color retouching and must experiment and progress with the industry.

Here is a quick review of the steps for retouching a color negative.

1. The lighter the area on a color negative, the deeper the shadow. This is the same technique used in black-and-white negative retouching.

2. Areas that are dense (strong highlights on print) can be corrected by blending the surrounding area with matching dye or pencil. (Remember the explanation from black-and-white retouching about stretching a material to make it thinner.)

3. Colors in the negative are approximately complementary to the colors in the original subject. Blemishes, lines, and wrinkles that show up in a variation of brown, red, or bluish tones are retouched with the similar color pencil for subduing or removing them altogether.

4. Veins, shadows from eyeglasses, dark hair growth, and even stray hairs against a bluish background (showing yellow-orange on the negative) are best retouched with either soft graphite or blue or black colorama pencils. For a larger area, the All Purpose Dye is well-liked by retouchers.

NOTE: The study of the color wheel (Color Plate 7) will be of great help to study the various complementary hues. Although the color wheel is not exact in color reproduction, one can observe its inner circle, compare it with the flesh tones of the color negative, and decide on the appropriate tone of color correction. Keep it on hand for frequent use.

Equipment

1. Retouching stand with 100-watt daylight blue bulb or 14-watt fluorescent cool white tube. As previously mentioned, some machine-operated retouching stands have the proper light already included. For those who use hand operated stands, the blue daylight bulb is very important. Only better hardware stores carry them.

2. Regular retouching graphites of various degrees with the addition of B, 2B, or 4B. Some retouchers also use silver graphites, but then it depends on the type of film surface being worked on. If your local camera or art stores do not have the pencils you need or have no selection in oil colors, write to The Pierce Company,

3701-R Nicollet Ave., Minneapolis, Minn. 55409, for a catalog of their retouching supplies. Only the K. West dyes and several other items mentioned in this book may be ordered directly from the National Retouchers Guild.

3. Colorama Color Graphites. These come in six colors and are the retouchers most useful tool for color negative retouching. The National Retouchers Guild has been importing them from Europe for the past few years. Although the demand is so heavy for them, it is surprising that art supply or camera stores still do not stock them. It's a good idea to request your local stores to order these ideal retouching and spotting graphites. There is no reason why a retoucher should whittle away on a wood pencil to get an awkward or broken point, slowing down his work and still needing endless resharpening. The colorama graphites fit into a regular graphite holder and may be sharpened to the finest point. They are actually watercolor pencils just as the Stabilo and Mongol pencils; their use in color spotting will be explained later. As a substitute for the above mentioned graphites, which come in red, brown, blue, yellow, black, and green, the following regular color pencils are acceptable: Eagle Prismacolor scarlet No. 922, indigo blue No. 901, dark brown No. 946; Mongol and Eberhard Faber red and blue. A set of Prismacolor pencils are necessary for spotting color prints, too.

4. Retouching fluid from retouching kit. K. West's retouching medium is specially prepared for color negatives and can be applied easily, which gives the negative a heavier "tooth." Items from other kits are absorbent cotton with skewer or applicators, tissue paper, and sable brushes. In addition to a couple of extra No. 000, No. 00, and No. 2 brushes, a palette should be added for keeping the brushes apart from the dark dyes and using them

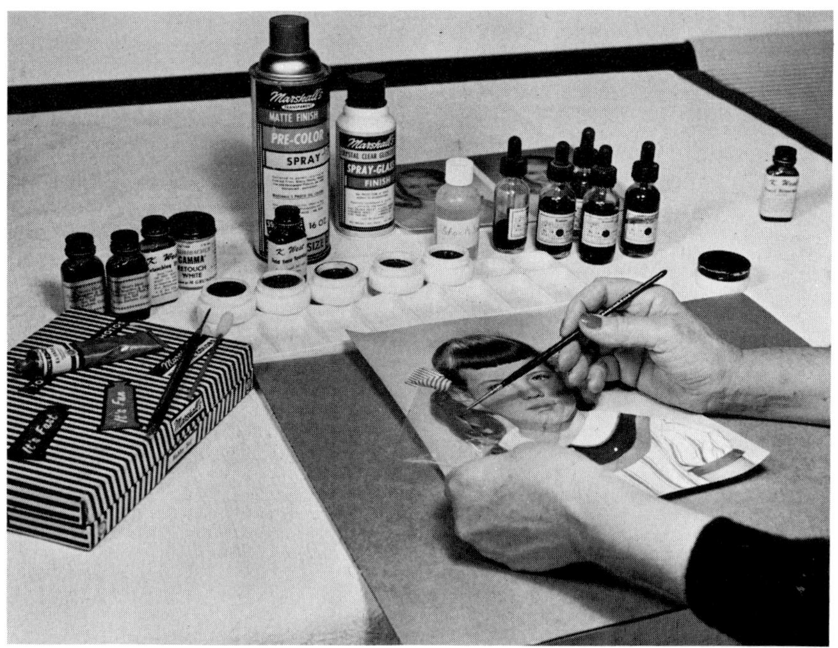

Fig. 70. Equipment for color retouching of prints. Utensils supplement those in previous illustration of retouching utensils. When testing to find proper dye color for spotting color prints, apply dye to pieces of glassine and hold close to print to determine exact match.

mainly for color dyes.

5. Set of negative retouching dyes for mixing your own. The Kodak retouching colors (formerly called Flexichrome) come in jars and are for either dry or wet retouching technique, more about them later. Additional brands are: Retouch Methods' set of color negative dyes, Marshall Co. color dyes. Buy dyes in small sizes; a little goes a long way, and normally a retoucher will want to experiment first before he decides on a larger supply.

6. If a proof is not available, a regular proof as for black-and-white retouching can be made. The process takes a little longer, but color negatives come out very nicely on Kodak Panalure paper.

Preparing Negative for Retouching

The *emulsion side* of a Kodacolor-X or Ektacolor *roll film* negative is facing you when the arrow is along the top edge and points to the right. The emulsion side of an Ektacolor *sheet film* negative is facing you when you hold the film so that the code notch is in the top right-hand corner. The Ektacolor *sheet film* negative has tooth on *both sides,* and one can retouch either side with dye, then dope, and apply color or graphite pencils. (This is the best film for the retoucher to work on.) Kodacolor-X and Ektacolor roll film have a very thin and slick surface, and retouching medium should be applied and blended down as gently as possible. Just wipe about three times over the surface with facial tissue in order not to rub it quite dry. On these smaller films, most of the corrective spotting and retouching is left for the print stage.

Retouching with Dye

Because of the variety of color film surfaces, it is again quite difficult to pinpoint a definite technique. Ektacolor *sheet film* takes dyes very well on both sides; the glossy side should always be worked first. Dope is applied after dye work is finished. Kodacolor-X and Ektacolor roll film, which have a slicker surface and are thinner to the touch than sheet film, require a more complex technique. Most often the slick surface will not hold the dye, and dye work must be performed on the emulsion side, which always shows a momentary discoloration. Because most color photography today is taken on the various roll films, the previously suggested testing of negatives should be made in order to keep the volume work uniform. There are a number of color retouching dyes available with specific instructions for their application.

Whichever dye the retoucher uses, one important aspect of working with the brush must be remembered. When retouching blemishes, lines, or other facial areas, a retoucher should use a dry brush that has been wiped once or twice over the back of the hand or on a piece of blotting paper.

The proper way to use a retouching brush is as follows: One should not bear down on the brush; the stroke should be a dabbing, constently moving one or an overlapping movement, working faster in a larger area, or slower for fine detail until the area is subdued.

When mixing dyes on a palette, if the drop by drop method is used, thin the solution with tap or distilled water. (Instead of water, some retouchers use denatured alcohol, because they found that it helps the dye adhere better to the emulsion.)

For the popular roll films many retouchers like the Kodak Retouch colors in jars. Buy a medium-size jar of this cake dye. Wet a No. 2 brush and brush it against the hard cake surface until you make a deep red color, add more water if necessary. Then take an eyedropper and transfer the liquid dye to the palette. Add a few dabs of either blue or neutral dye to the red, testing the dye frequently on the discard negative until you achieve the proper hue. When you get the correct hue, make a little more solution and put it in a small bottle with an eyedropper. Label the jar with a white sticker and paint a streak onto the label. This will help identify the dye at a later date.

For those who like premixed dyes, the new "K" dyes I and II are worth trying. Number I has a bluish-violet tint, and number II tends toward reddish-brown. Color dye Flesh II can also be used, as well as Gold Tone Spotter and All Purpose Dye. With this wide selection of dyes, the color retoucher has all the necessary materials for doing an excellent color retouching job.

By all means test the dye first on a discard negative or a glassine envelope to see whether you have the right tone. Hold the negative by the corner in the glassine envelope rather than placing it on the negative mask on the retouching stand. This allows for freer movement in turning the negative, and helps to lighten your touch.

On small faces in a photograph there is very little that can be done with either dye or pencil. Dye is not recommended at all and only very obvious spots or lines can be lightly touched up with pencil. It is regretable that photographers do not use up more of the negative area for portraiture, so that there is enough space to spot the print if necessary. The retoucher can often perform the impossible, but he cannot perform miracles!

When dye retouching is finished, the negative is doped, on both sides if skin texture is rough, and placed immediately in a sleeve or mask to protect it from dust and fingerprints.

NOTE: Do not remove specks or dust from color negative with your fingers. The negative surface is so sensitive that the roughness of a fingertip can scratch it. Use either a soft brush or a whiff with tissue paper to remove an imbedded speck.

Retouching with Pencils

Before we try to retouch the flesh tones on a color negative, we must bear in mind that the human face reflects a multitude of hues, from the palest yellow to rose and from brown to bluish-grey. In this respect only, color negative retouching is different from black-and-white retouching. The technique of the stroke is the same for both, but for color the retoucher must interchange his color pencils and various plain graphites with respect to the particular need of the portrait. With a little practice it is quite surprising how quickly one can learn to read a color negative. Greenish flesh tone on a color negative indicates that the subject has a ruddy complexion; the paler the skin tone on the positive, the more bluish-violet it will be on the negative. This is quite simple to remember, and all corrections follow this example. Until some new medium of texture correction is invented, the color pencil and the graphite is the retoucher's best friend.

Pick out the deepest blemishes and lines and correct them with the red pencil. Do not try to eliminate the blemishes altogether by pressing down on the negative. Instead, gradually soften them with a soft graphite or black, brown, or blue colorama. Go lightly over all the greenish spots and continually interchange the graphites until the spot or line blends in with the original color hue on the negative. Additional retouching can be done on the base side (glossy surface).

Always use color pencils before applying the graphite pencils, and plan to *underretouch* the negative. In other words, minimize rather than maximize the area you plan to retouch, because the natural color of the print compensates for color hues. Overretouching causes the spots or areas to become blue on the final print. Also, pressure on the thin negative penetrates the top color layer and can cause a color shift when the negative is printed.

For obstinate and deep pimples or blemishes, which appear as a clear spot (almost black on the proof), take the abrading tool, turn the negative to the glossy side, and gently scratch (not dig) the spot. The gelatine will either cover the transparent area altogether, or a light touch with color or B graphite will cover it up.

This is pencil color retouching in a nutshell, and different techniques are only variations on a theme.

NOTE: Abrading tools are obtainable in better camera stores. It is not necessary to have an electric machine for it. Usually, an abrading tool comes with the machine-operated stand, but it can also be worked by hand. Never use it on the emulsion side, because it will ruin the surface, neither should it be used as an etching tool.

Retouching Negative Faults

HIGHLIGHTS

If there is a green area between highlights one can blend them by applying either the terracotta pencil, reddish dye (Flesh II), or soft graphite. A catchlight in the eyes can be restored by applying a touch of Kodak Opaque from a very fine brush, or by using the Colorama black pencil. Moisten the pencil with saliva and apply it to the film. Black Colorama pencils also work ideally as a substitute for a B or 2B pencil on *negatives and prints.*

SHADOWS

Areas of negative may be intensified with color dyes or pencils. If, for instance, a dress is red and the shadow is too dark, one can apply a green dye (which is the color on the negative) and minimize the shadow.

PINHOLES AND SCRATCHES

Pinholes (caused by dust specks) appear on the finished print as dark spots and should always be removed right on the color negative before printing. Since etching cannot be performed on color film, the negative can be spotted in several ways. Either use Opaque White or black in liquid or dry form (Kodak, Marshall, Spotone) applied with a fine brush or a Colorama black pencil moistened with saliva, which also makes a good spotting. This will appear as a light speck on the print, which can be easily matched to the right color tone with dyes or pencil.

Some retouchers can handle a stylus or abrading needle slightly off-center of the pinhole, pushing toward the center to move the minute portion of the base (film grain) over the pinhole. It will hold the light in that area. Do not use a needle on the emulsion side. The first technique is preferable.

Minor scratches can be removed with Kodak Abrasive Reducer. We mentioned this product in connection with rubbing down strong densities on black-and-white negatives and applying over etched areas when working with the condenser enlarger (Chapter 3).

Pick up a small amount on a tuft of cotton and rub it against a glass or smooth surface (glassine or cellophane will do). Gently apply it to the area and then smooth it down with clean cotton. Too much pressure can cause penetration of the top yellow layer, causing damage.

Removing Pencil Retouching

Pencil retouching may be removed with an application of the regular retouching medium. However, if the negative has been worked over a couple of times, it will not take pencil any more. Kodak Print Lacquer Thinner (Type 2), denatured alcohol, or carbon tetrachloride will remove all traces of dope and leave the negative clean.

Removing Dye Retouching

Dye retouching can be removed entirely by washing the negative in running water for several minutes and drying it in the usual manner. Local reduction of dye on the glossy (base) side can best be subdued by using a moistened cotton swab or skewer. (Refer to neutral dye-retouching on black-and-white negatives). Allow the negative to dry before continuing to retouch.

Points to Remember About Color Negative Retouching

1. Apply dye first on the base, or the emulsion side if it is roll film. Sometimes an application of dope on the slick emulsion side holds the dye better. It is up to the individual to try several techniques and use whatever works best for him.

2. After doping the negative, use color pencils before retouching with graphites.

3. Try to match the retouched area in tone and density with the negative.

4. Neutralize green with red, yellow with blue, and other colors with a combination of neutral tones. (K. West dyes can be mixed with other colors for accurate tone.)

5. Remember: An application of the *same color as the negative* will lighten the area in hue; just as the complementary color neutralizes, so the same color reduces density. In other words, if a dress is red and the shadow is too dark, one can apply a green dye (the color on the negative) and minimize the shadow.

6. Etching cannot be done on color negatives. Pinholes are either removed with an abrading tool or spotted with opaque.

7. Keep your retouching brushes very clean. Have a dish of water at your side to rinse the brush from one dye to another.

8. Fingerprints can be removed by rubbing the edges of the negative between clean tissue paper (Kleenex), or if necessary by adding a touch of dope and blending it out.

9. Keep informed of new products or techniques by writing to Eastman Kodak Co., Rochester, N.Y. 14650, or to other companies who produce retouching and spotting dyes for their pamphlets. A professional retoucher should subscribe to either of the two photography magazines: *The Rangefinder*, 1300 North Wilton Place, Hollywood, Calif. 90028 or *The Professional Photographer*, Oak Leaf Commons, Des Plains, Ill. 60018. Frequently, there are articles on new retouching methods published in these magazines, and for a retoucher who does not have much contact with photographers, reading up on news in the photo business will keep him up to date and well-informed about his profession. These magazines are also the best source of advertising one's services throughout the country.

CHAPTER 11

Retouching Color Transparencies

Of all the kinds of color retouching, retouching transparencies has always been my favorite. I was introduced to this work back in 1945, when only a few retouchers knew the method. Most of them were employed in Hollywood film studios, worked behind closed doors, and guarded their secret jealously. I needed only one lesson (for which I paid a tidy sum) to find out why it was kept a secret. The technique was so simple that one demonstration sufficed to start me on the road to color retouching.

Later on, as an instructor at the Fred Archer School in Los Angeles, I had the opportunity to apply my knowledge in helping students with their color retouching problems. Great progress has been made in color photography in recent years, bringing faster films, automatic processing, and further innovation. Yet, to my delight, the technique of retouching transparencies remains the same. I can sit down to a color transparency today and correct it the same way I did twenty years ago.

Color transparencies are again becoming popular, and the retoucher who has a little knowledge of coloring, combined with the various dye retouching techniques previously mentioned, will find color transparency retouching easy and lucrative. One cannot ruin a transparency, particularly on sheet film, which has an easy-to-work surface. Here too there are a few fundamental rules: dyes are applied first; doping and pencil retouching are performed later; film should be kept free of finger marks; a paper corner should be used.

Transparency corrections offer a much wider scope of visual improvement because of the direct color that can be intensified, changed, or reduced. A very informative source of other color dye techniques for the novice can be found in *Hand Coloring Your Photographs With Oils and Dyes* (Amphoto), in which detailed instructions on coloring and dye color techniques are fully explained. In this book we are more concerned with the application of colors as they apply to the retouching procedure.

Equipment

The necessary equipment is the same as for retouching color negatives. One should have a set of color dyes (Photo Retouch Colors by Marshall or Eastman Kodak Co. are good), and a few assorted color retouching pencils. The colors already mentioned are aniline dyes that are sold in bottles.

However, water colors are also quite suitable for working on color film and on color prints. Water colors come in opaque form or in soluble form, as dye-coated leaflets.

The dye pigments on paper (leaflets) are very inexpensive. Because of their maximum color strength only a tiny amount is needed to make a color solution. It has often been asked whether aniline or water color dyes are permanent. *There is no permanent* fade-proof water or aniline dye. This is probably the reason why the most beautiful water color paintings are never valued as much as oil paintings. However, the color applied to transparencies remains unchanged for many years, as it is not too exposed to light. If color prints are restored with dyes and then sprayed, they will also be better protected against fading.

At a minimum cost the retoucher can make water color solutions that in color and hue may be superior to anything he could buy in bottles.

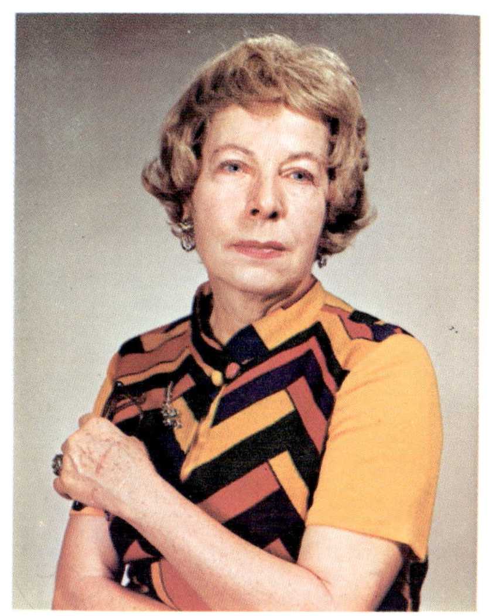

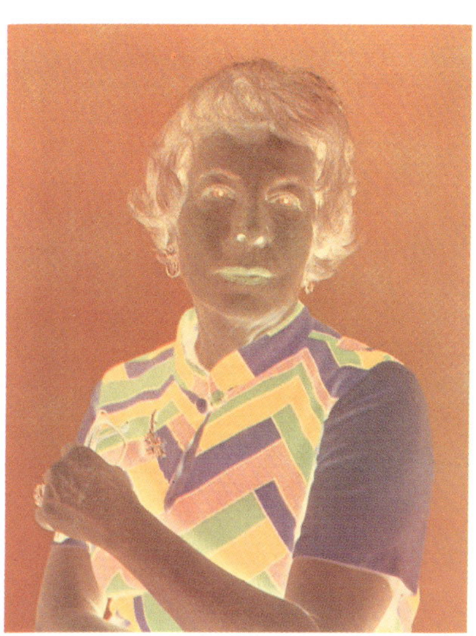

Plates 1 and 2. Original unretouched color print and negative.

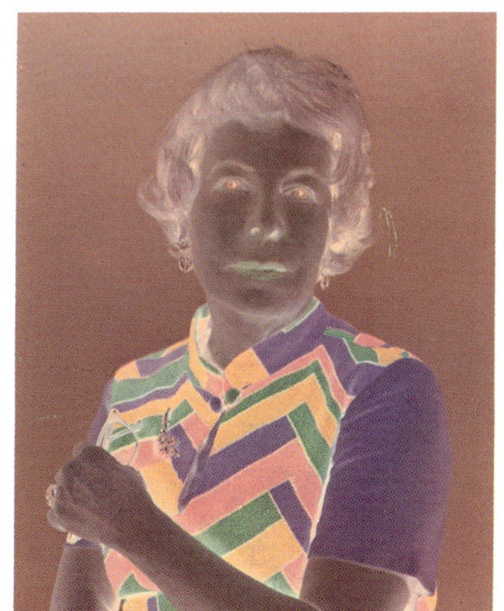

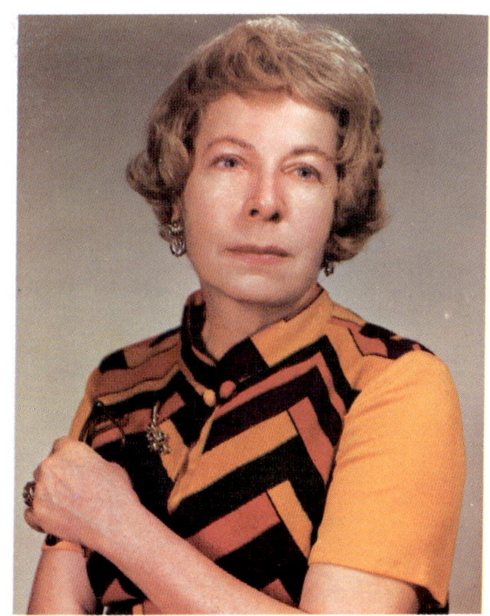

Plates 3 and 4. Retouched negative and print.

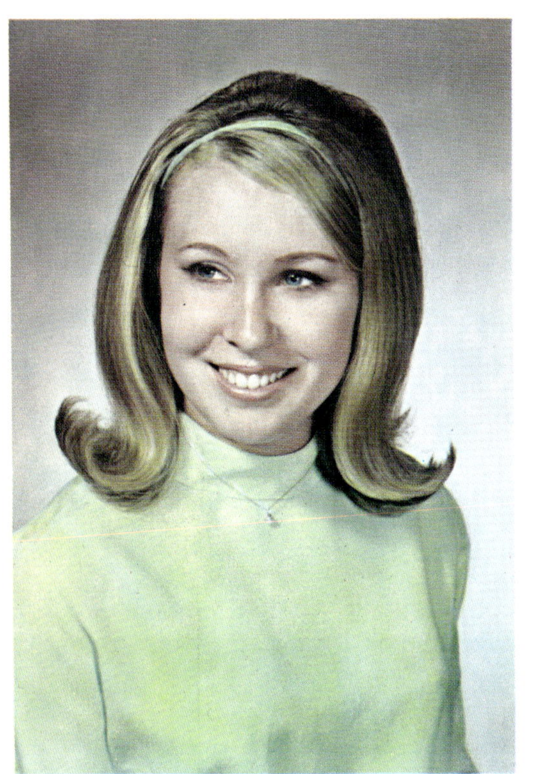

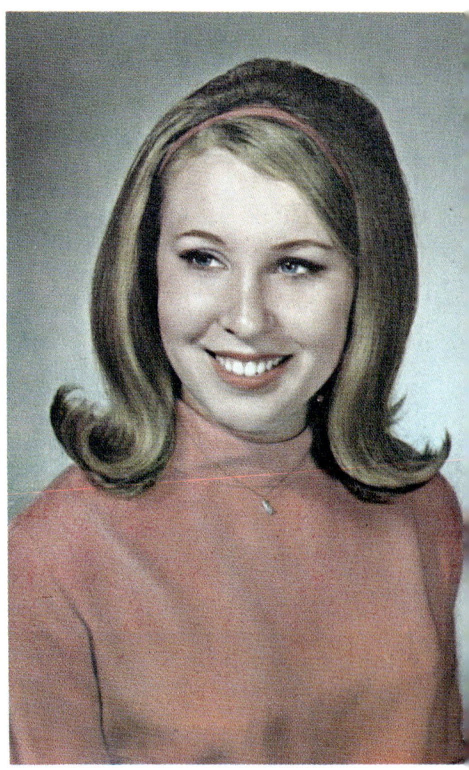

Plates 5 and 6. Observe improved color achieved by application of dry Flexichrome dyes with cotton tuft.

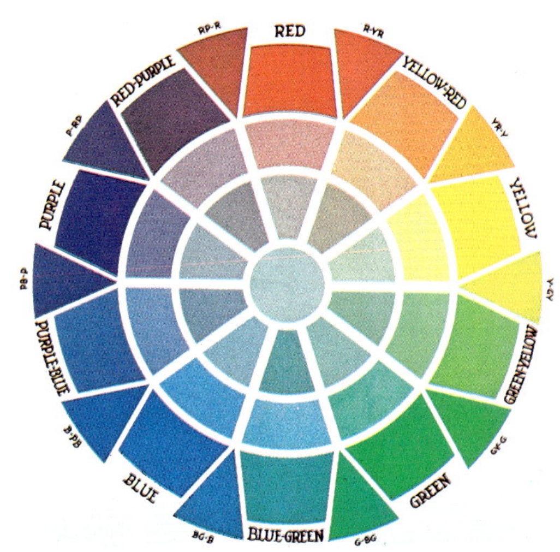

Plate 7. Color wheel.

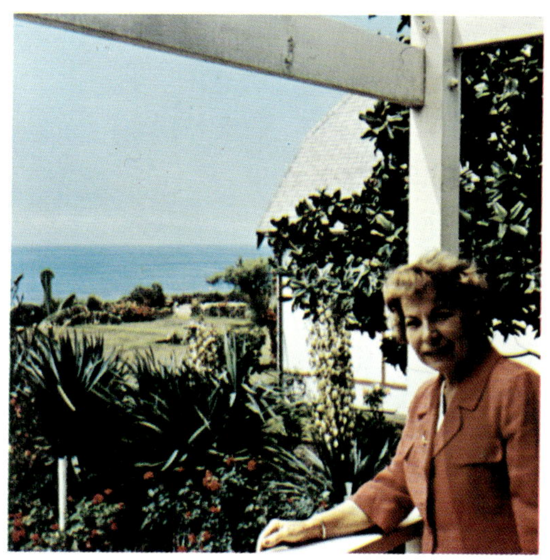

Plate 8. Unretouched color transparency.

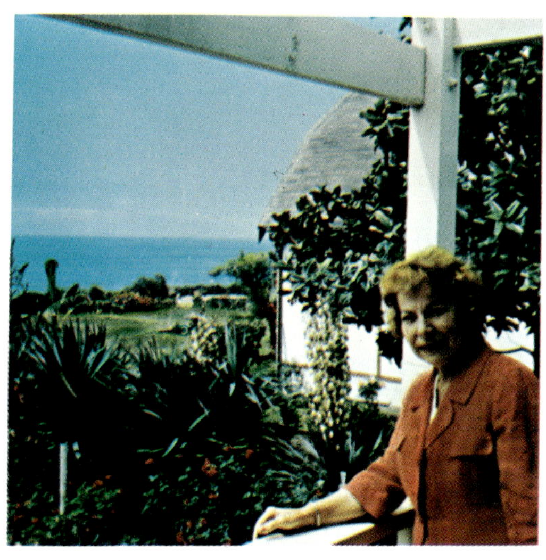

Plate 9. Color has been improved with an application of dye on transparency. Result is even tone of red dress, greener grass, grayed roof, lightened hair, and darkened pole in foreground.

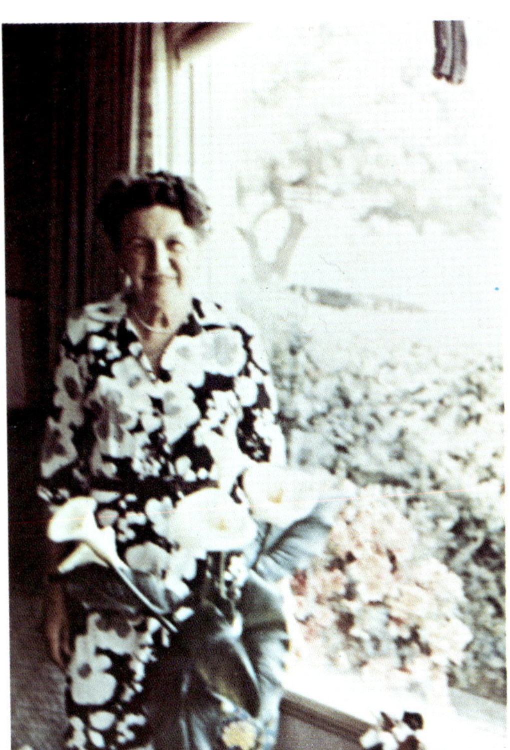

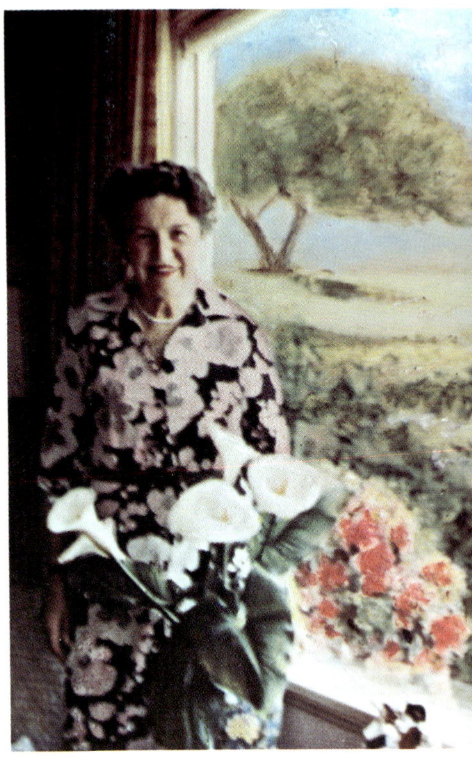

Plate 10. Original color print, faded and lacking detail.

Plate 11. Improved print. Oil color technique was used to cover up tassel in window and generally improve picture. For protection, picture was sprayed with Spray-Glass.

Eastman Kodak Company makes a set of twelve strips that can be bought in art stores and will suffice for average coloring or spotting problems.

Peerless Watercolors or Nicholson's Watercolors are brand names for these watercolors or leaflets. They come in dozens of colors, but are rather difficult to obtain. For the average retoucher, the set of twelve retouch colors by Marshall's or Retouch Methods Co. will provide a perfect scope for mixing the proper dyes. Since these dyes are also used for color print spotting and the method of applying them is so similar to the method used for applying them to the film surface of the transparency or direct color print, the following techniques can be simply interchanged. Only the application of dyes to large areas of clothes or background differs from print correction. The size of the color transparency and the size of an 8″ x 10″ color print cannot be treated the same way.

Preparing Color Dyes

If a color leaflet is used, cut a piece of one or two different colors off and place them in a shallow glass with two ounces of water for a stock solution. Use distilled water, and add a drop or two of Photo-Flo or Pako-Wett.

About ten or twelve of the most frequently used colors ought to be prepared as standard stock solutions. Kodak colors have perforated color stamps; Peerless color sheets have to be cut in about one-inch squares and placed in a shallow glass with one or two ounces of the stock solution previously mentioned: distilled water, with a few drops of Photo-Flo or Pako-Wett.

With a skewer or orange-stick keep stirring the color stamp around till all color is loosened and the strip is clear. Discard the paper. Have a few small bottles on hand. Small cosmetic bottles are practical. Either pour or use a dropper to put the solution into them. Close the caps tightly and label them with a strip of white paper on which the name of the color is marked and on which a little color from the bottle has been smeared with the brush so that the hue can be recognized at a glance.

The same procedure may be applied to the bottled aniline dyes by Kodak, Marshall, or another company. Always use an eye dropper for mixing colors and test the color on white paper before applying, or apply first on cellophane (glassine) right over the color transparency to see if the color is right.

White *cannot* be achieved with these dyes. The only way this can be done is by using the opaque white or other opaque colors (Grumbacher or another make).

Application

Before starting to add dye to a color transparency, the retoucher must remember to apply the solution in weak applications at all times and to achieve stronger shades by repeated strokes. Beautiful effects may be obtained by applying various color washes. This is particularly necessary in a color transparency of a landscape or a still life. If, for example, one wants to create an effect of various shades of green (on grass or trees), one can apply a yellowish color first, then go over it with green in the brown areas and violet in the shaded areas. In other words, always remember to *start with very light hues* and continue to deepen them either with the same color or with variations of darker colors. *This is the whole trick to color technique.* (See Color Plates 8 and 9.)

Retouching Skin Tones

Only skin tones of pale hue can be corrected; dark tones can only be neutralized. More about that later. Colors that appear dark on a transparency, whether on skin, dress, or anything else, cannot be made lighter because of the transparency of color dyes, which do not show over dark tones. Sometimes the bleaching process with skewer and swab is advisable. (The process would be the same as in bleaching on color prints.) There are at present selective dye bleaches for Kodak Ektacolor professional paper that are used by photographers in the laboratory in connection with developing the films. The retoucher will hardly be called upon to do the bleaching of color layers. He will be concerned primarily with reducing or spotting out that which can be done over the retouching desk. Anyone wishing to get the formulas for preparing Kodak selective bleaches should write for pamphlet No. E-70, in which the procedure is expertly presented.

The supplies and products in photography are continually undergoing changes. Sometimes before a book on a specific product is published a new product has appeared and another one is off the market. Making frequent visits to his camera store and attending conventions will keep the professional photographer or retoucher well-informed on available products.

PROCEDURE

Apply dye on the glossy side of the transparency. In order to judge which color should be used for correcting a pale yellow skin tone, for example, the following suggestion will help. The first skin color one should see is a pinkish-brown. Since the color on the transparency (or for that matter on a color print) is already a pale yellow, mix the lightest tint of a little red and warm brown to make a very pale mixture. Then take a piece of glassine, clear film, or celluloid and apply this mixture with a No. 00 brush. If the color is right, start applying it in light, quick movements on the transparency to parts of the face where color is needed. Should the tint be too strong or too pink in comparison with the skin tone, change it by diluting it with an eyedropper on a metal palette or saucer. A touch of Neutral Tint or green will neutralize the red. For larger areas a fine cotton-tipped skewer, wiped off against the bottle neck, will not make streaks.

The tint must look natural at all times. Have another skewer with a clean wet tip ready, and work gently over the dyed area to even up strokes. It is surprising what a few brush strokes will do to a washed-out skin tone on a transparency or color print, and what a help it is in getting prints of perfect color value. All these color corrections are made in less time than it takes to read the instructions. The most time-consuming part is the preparation of the dye. A flesh color is more difficult to prepare than any other color. K. West's Ideal Flesh No. I will be a time saver, and will provide a good soft skin tone.

Eyes, lips, and eyebrows on a transparency should be done with the fine brush. Application of color to a dress or other objects may be easier to do with a swab or skewer, wrapped as illustrated in Fig. 14. It is not easy to make a tight and fine skewer tip, neither too bulky nor too thin. The special hazard in a too-thin tip is that the stick may be exposed and damage the film or paper. It takes practice to get it just right.

After dye has been applied to parts of the film and dried thoroughly, one can apply dope to the emulsion side of the color transparency and work with regular retouching pencils or color pencils. If highlights are still too strong, one can tone them down with color pencil. A blemish may be subdued by retouching *around* it with graphite or a pencil of a suitable color, thus making it less obvious.

Dye can be removed by local swabbing, or can be entirely removed by rinsing the negative off under tap water and drying it in the usual manner. Pencil retouching is cleaned off with retouching medium, turpentine, or carbon tetrachloride.

Commercial Work

Color transparencies are being used increasingly to advertise everything under the sun. In scenic pictures a thin application of blue will enhance the sky, touches of red will make rooftops redder, green will make grass greener.

Catalog color-layouts are enhanced with stronger color hues for better printing value. The commercial photographer can save himself time and money by knowing how to enhance his color transparencies for better effect, and the retoucher should utilize every opportunity to acquire transparencies or color negatives on which to practice. Suggestions on how to obtain them are given in Chapter 13.

The retoucher who has a set of Kodak Flexichrome colors may also use them for retouching large areas on transparencies. If, for instance, a sky should be a deeper blue, rub a tuft of cotton (or the tip of the swab) over the color in the jar and apply the color to the base side of the transparency with small circular motions. Blend any streaks very lightly with a fresh piece of cotton. The method of Flexichrome application would be the same as in color print retouching, Chapter 12. Overlapped areas are cleaned off by using denatured alcohol on the swabs. This dry method is convenient for one who would like to experiment with diluted dyes and also see the effect of the rubbed-in dye. Although the effect achieved with the dry method is satisfactory, the liquid colors are always more intense.

Bleaching

If possible, one should refrain from bleaching any film surface. However, in an emergency a transparency area can be bleached (in contrast to the color negative, on which spot bleaching cannot be done).

Stock Solutions for Spot Bleaching

(May also be used for color prints)

Solution A: Water, 100 cc.
Potassium permanganate, 5.25 grams

Solution B: Distilled water, 100 cc.
Sulfuric acid concentrated, 3.20 cc.

Mix equal quantities of A and B solutions and apply with a No. 0 or No. 1 brush. An inexpensive brush will do, because the solution spoils the hairs after a short time. Moisten the brush to a fine point and lightly touch the spot. The solution should not spread; if it does, a bleached ring will appear. You will notice how the tone of the film changes to a brownish hue.

Wash the brush well in water, or if you like, use another fine brush and moisten it in the following solution:

Distilled water, 100 cc.
Sodium bisulfate, 1 gram

Apply it lightly to the discolored spot and observe how the brown stain vanishes. Use the solution sparingly. A little swabbing with a cotton tip moistened in clear water will remove any solution that remains. Let the transparency dry thoroughly before touching it up with color dye or pencil. (This technique applies to color prints also.)

NOTE: Bleaching is done on the *emulsion* (matte) side of a transparency. Dye should be applied to the *glossy* side because on Ektacolor Print Film the emulsion side discolors when moistened. Kodacolor film accepts dyes on both sides without discoloration. In both instances retouching medium may be applied to both sides after all dye or bleaching is done.

Opaquing

Color transparencies used for photomontage or for commercial purposes can be opaqued in the same manner as black-and-white negatives. The original picture can be restored by washing the transparency under running water.

CHAPTER 12

Retouching Color Prints

The technique is very similar to the retouching of color transparencies, with the added possibility of using transparent oil colors. With the increased use of small film there is going to be an ever-growing demand for good color print finishers because there is little opportunity for retouching on the color negative.

Retouching or spotting color prints of any type is surprisingly easy if one knows what technique is appropriate for a particular problem. Again, we shall try to simplify the evaluation of corrective methods.

1. If print corrections are only necessary in small areas, the "dry brush" dye application or color pencil is best.

2. If a print requires large areas of color intensification on face, dress, or background, the Flexichrome dry method is recommended.

3. If a color print requires rather drastic changes in color and practically the whole print could stand improvement, the oil color technique will be the answer.

Equipment

To the equipment one has acquired for negative color and transparency retouching, one should add Marshall's Photo-Oil color outfit, Marshall's Pre-Color Spray, Pro-Tek-To Spray,

Kodak Print Lacquer Matte or Getzol's Type C Matte Lacquer. For a glossy finish one should have on hand Marshall's Spray-Glass, Kodak Print Lacquer Clear, or other makes of varnishes available in photo supply stores and art shops.

It is usually up to the spotter or retoucher to determine which make he prefers. The Eastman Kodak Co. and the John G. Marshall Mfg. Co. (manufacturer of Webster's dye) have at present a wide range of liquid photo-retouch colors. As mentioned before, these colors are all aniline dyes, and it is important with these, as with any products, to know how and where to use them. Once any technique of color retouching is grasped, the name of the retouching product used makes little difference, because all these companies have brought their products to the same high level of perfection.

In addition to dyes and oil colors, the following are necessary: a drawing board; a white metal or plastic watercolor palette or saucers, for mixing colors and washing the brushes (a plastic egg-container makes an inexpensive and convenient utensil with twelve good-sized wells); fine sable brushes from previous equipment.

The retouching area should be well illuminated. There is no substitute for plain daylight. If artificial light is used, the General Electric Deluxe Cool White fluorescent lamp (in fixtures), Macbeth Avlite, Sylvania Deluxe Cool White, or Mazda blue daylight bulb will serve for viewing approximate color quality.

Kodak Flexichrome colors are available in red, green, blue, cyan, magenta, yellow, neutral, flesh basis, and brown. *It is important not to mix them for the dry or wet method.* Colors that are applied with a cotton swab should not be dampened with a water brush because the dye retains moisture and would smear when used for the cotton application.

In order to save money, when color spotting is not done in a photo lab, I would suggest scooping out a half-jar of each color and placing the colors in individual wells on the watercolor palette, where they will be used only with brushes. The color remaining in the jars should be kept strictly for use with cotton swabs or tufts.

With the use of Flexichrome dyes one should have a small bottle of anhydrous denatured alcohol (Quixol, manufactured by Commercial Solvents Corporation, 260 Madison Ave., New York, N. Y.). Other Eastman Kodak products in connection with working on Ektacolor prints will be found in their pamphlet No. E-70. However, I found that Marshall's Extender will perform similar cleaning action. (See section on "Flexichrome Application.")

A spacious table is essential, because working with dyes and colors always becomes a little messy and cramped space causes spilling of dyes and other unnecessary complications. A magnifying glass (either one from your retouching stand or one with a handle) should be on hand for detailed work.

Procedure

Make sure the print surface is absolutely clean and dry. Use anhydrous denatured alcohol on a tuft of surgical-grade absorbent cotton. It is the best for use in *all* techniques where cotton is being used. Apply lightly and burnish the print surface with another tuft of dry cotton. Press softly, otherwise you scratch the surface; then color sets into the area and cannot be removed. I often prefer just a gentle buffing with dry cotton. As when handling negatives and color transparencies, one should use cotton gloves or a blotter or white paper between hand and print.

For spotting always *use liquid dyes first,* then apply pencils, oil colors, or sprays. This is very important to remember.

Retouching Small Areas and Spots

Mix a few drops of color-retouching dyes on the palette or, if you use Flexichrome, pick up a little color and mix it with the prepared stock solution mentioned before. The Neutral Dye reduces the brilliance of pure colors. K. West Dye mixes very well. As in all color dyes, the color should be weak and density increased as necessary. For spotting out or improving skin tones, you will find the Ideal Flesh I and Flesh II the best color dye formulated for this purpose. The carefully pre-mixed dye will save time and testing, and it flows easily on any print surface without leaving streaks or a trace of its application. It is available only through the National Retouchers Guild, Santa Barbara, Calif.

Stroke the brush with the color mixture over a white blotter, newsprint, or facial tissue to remove excess moisture, and apply the almost-dry brush to spots or small areas to be retouched.

Quick blotting of a retouched area helps to maintain control of the density. The technique of keeping the brush stroke from overlapping into the surrounding area is generally rapidly mastered by the spotter. Too-strong highlights can be spotted out with a few touches, exaggerated laughlines subdued, and highlights from eyeglasses toned down, often with just one dip into the dye. Spotting of background or matching light areas is easy when the glassine is superimposed on the print for testing.

Larger areas may also be intensified with liquid dyes. In this case a swab is preferable, or a round sable brush No. 1 or No. 3. The application of a more loaded brush is particularly appropriate when color is being added to hair or on a dress or when one is blurring an object in the background. The movement should be loose and quick. By keeping the color very weak, the strokes blend into each other without showing streaks.

NOTE: For the beginner it is always recommended to start color spotting or retouching on smaller prints and areas. The handling of larger areas requires a definite skill. The main problem in handling dyes is the accuracy of stroke, avoiding overlapping into another color area. If more than one print has to be spotted, it is best to apply one color to all the prints in order to keep a uniform tone. Tacking the print down is not advisable in color spotting, as it is easier to work by turning the print around for a better approach to the areas to be colored.

Retouching Color Prints

Spots: The dark spots on the print are caused by pinholes in the color negative. The spotting on color negatives was explained in Chapter 10. Taking care of pinholes in the beginning will avoid complications in print spotting. On prints made from negatives where head sizes were small and retouching of lines and blemishes insufficient, you must spot the dark lines or facial marks with an opaque color.

1. The quickest and probably most original way to do this is to make the following application on an unsprayed or sprayed color print. Place a dab of Marshall's Flesh or Basic Flesh on a piece of wax paper, and add to it a drop of Titanium or Flake White. Then mix the two colors together. (For deeper flesh lines any of the flesh shadow oil colors should work.) Take a fine brush (not your regular brush for dye work), any No. 00 or 000, and apply the mixed color in a fine stroke *right over* the dark line or blemish. Again, a piece of transparent paper is good for testing the right color, and a piece of cotton will remove the color if it is the wrong shade. Dab gently over the area until the bluish tone or speck disappears. With a little experimentation the spotter will find this particular technique to be a good answer to the problem of volume print spotting. Also, this technique gives you the advantage of being able to work on the unsprayed print as opposed to other methods in which the print must be sprayed before and after the application of dyes. Of course, other corrections such as filling out hair or covering it up against the background can be performed with other oil colors. Be sure to let the print dry for several hours before spraying; otherwise the oil will "run" or discolor.

2. Another method well worth trying out and with astounding results, is the use of regular *fluid make-up* products, which are sold in variety or department stores. Get the inexpensive ones in tubes or jars; two or three shades from light to dark will match the average skin tone of the color print. Squeeze the tube to remove the oil from the top, and place a dab of color on a piece of wax paper. You can mix two or three shades of this regular make-up to the right tone and actually perform a "*make-up*" right on the print. The main difference between this method and the one mentioned above is that for this one you must matte-spray the print *before* the make-up application. In my experimentation it was not necessary to spray the print again, however, it is up to the spotter to decide whether additional spraying is necessary. Unsatisfactory work may be cleaned off with Marshall's *Extender* before starting again.

3. The use of color pencils over a lacquered surface is another method of color print retouching. The recent product called Retouchable Matte by Dale Color, Inc., P.O. Box 460, Bloomington, Ill. 61701, is perfect for this technique. They also produce a complete Retouch Kit, which contains every color pencil necessary for black-and-white and color print retouching. Dale Color Inc. publishes an informative booklet on color retouching techniques with pencils. You can write to them for more information concerning this material and also for price information on single color pencils. Of course, many of these brand-name color pencils may be obtained in art supply stores, but a complete kit gives one the incentive to try various methods of print correction. The Colorama graphites are also very practical for detail spotting, and a touch of the black or blue colorama, moistened with saliva, will touch up a most obstinate spot in a very dark area.

The most useful color pencil that will cover up skin faults is the Prismacolor No. 939 Flesh and the No. 927 Flesh. One can correct a wrong color with a rubber eraser and with repeated application of Retouchable Matte or McDonalds Matte Lacquer.

Scratches: Surface scratches that have removed one or more dye layers of the emulsion can be repaired by dye application with a fine brush. Dye of the correct concentration and hue should be added to the scratched area in the proper order.

1. The Ektacolor print consists of three layers: cyan (blue) is the top layer. It is followed by magenta (red), and yellow. If a scratch appears red, the magenta layer has been scratched and thus an application of the cyan (blue) will normalize the color. A scratch that appears yellow indicates the removal of both red and blue color layers. First the blue and then the red color (in the proper density) have to be applied. Let the negative dry after each color application. If the scratch shows by reflected light, an application of any of the lacquers already mentioned is necessary.

2. I have found another way to overcome scratches in a hurry. I spray the print with matte lacquer, let it dry, and then simply apply the retouching pencil and different color pencils to match the scratch as it spreads over various color areas. Then I spray the print again with glossy or matte spray, which will restore the surface to what it should be.

Summary: From the above mentioned ways to correct a print, it is obvious that there should not be any more discards, now that the spotter knows how to "doctor-up" a print to make it salable. Because color printing is a very complex process and involves large sums of money if not perfectly executed, a good print spotter has reached an important place in the industry if he can prevent the extra expense of reprinting or discarding for the photo lab or studio.

The following list provides a summary of the utensils available for color print spotting:

1. Color dyes, preferably those used on clear prints (unlacquered).
2. Lead pencils or Colorama graphites, best applied over matte prints, as all the following pencils should be used.
3. Verithin or Stabilo pencils are hard color pencils and useful for detail work.
4. Prismacolor are medium soft pencils and have the flesh to brown range for covering lines, and so on.

5. Grease pencils are convenient for covering larger areas or objects in the background.

6. Pastel pencils are better than pastel sticks and can be blended well with swabsticks or fingers. (The oil coloring method is preferred.)

7. Transparent oils give an unlimited scope to corrections and changes on a print. They become opaque by adding *white* to any color.

8. Application of Flexichrome (Kodak Retouch Colors) or the use of Hibadye photo colors , (Jamieson Products Co.), which have many applications in print finishing.

9. Several brands of spray lacquers from matte to glossy.

Because each product has its particular method of application, and describing every single technique would only confuse the reader, the addresses of suppliers of all retouching materials are listed in the back of this book. Reading the suggestions and directions about *how and where* to use an individual product is an advantage to the buyer, who usually pays little attention to the fine print on the label.

Neutralizing Off-Color Areas

(On a Color Print or Transparency)

Dark color areas of a print cannot be lightened, but by neutralizing them the tone will be changed. If you use the complementary color, an off-color area will improve in appearance. For example, red will be neutralized by a faint application of cyan (bluish-green), green by magenta (red), blue by orange, yellow by purple. These colors may be applied by either a liquid or dry method (Flexichrome method, follows shortly), whichever application is practical for a specific problem.

Removing Dye

Removing liquid dyes from color prints is not very easy. Alcohol will not work. Kodak Photo-Flo 200 solution can be

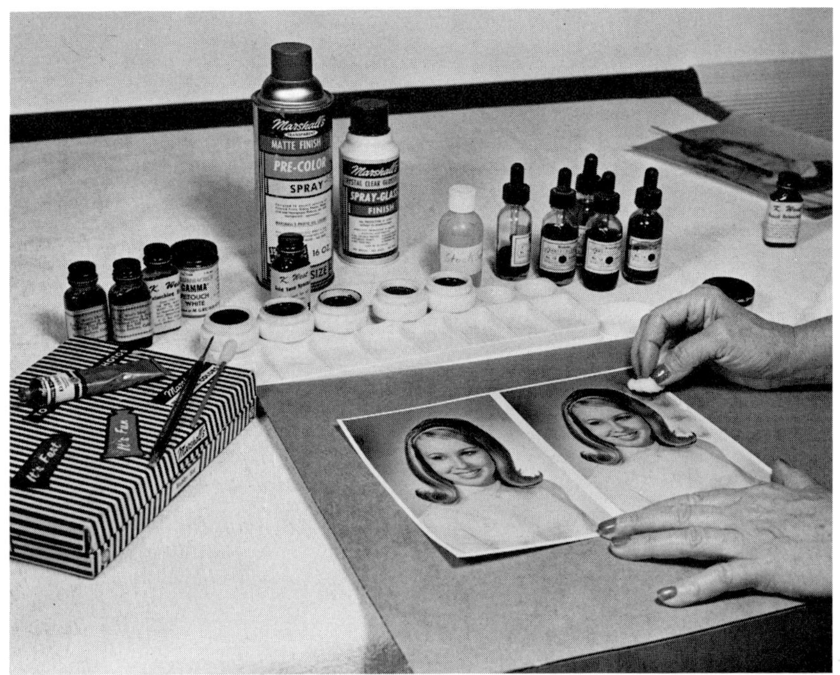

Fig. 71. Application of dry Flexichrome dyes with cotton tuft. Observe improved color illustration of example in Color Plates 5 and 6.

applied carefully to the particular area with either a swab or a brush. Within a half-minute blot off the area with newsprint or white blotter and with a solution containing *equal parts* of Kodak Stabilizer CP-5 (or Ektaprint C Stabilizer) and water, then reapply. Allow print to dry thoroughly before continuing with spotting.

NOTE: Try washing a print. Sometimes dye is nicely subdued. First try it on a discard print.

Flexichrome Dry Method

Of all color retouching techniques this is the easiest method for one who knows little about coloring techniques. The skill is quickly acquired. When one is able to intensify or change a weak color in any area, the work becomes fascinating and rewarding. One can experiment with various colors, adding and changing till the desired effect is achieved, before making the retouching permanent. Even the glossiest prints may be changed without losing the glossy surface. (Fig. 72, Colors Plates 5 and 6.)

Take a tuft of dry cotton, breathe on the Flexichrome dye in the jar a few times, and rub some dye on a piece of cotton. Apply in circular motions, being careful to stay in the area you wish to intensify or change. Take another clean tuft and very lightly blend down the streaks of the first application. If highlights have to be picked out of color overlapped into another color, use a dry swab and take out more color. Also, a little Extender (Marshall's) on the swab will clean edges or remove part of the entire application. Anhydrous alcohol is also recommended for correcting or removing colors.

To build up additional density apply steam and let the dye set. A small, inexpensive electric vaporizer is recommended for one who is going to use the dry method to a larger extent. The print should be subjected to steam for only a few seconds. In an emergency even the steam from a tea kettle might work. Spraying the color print after a Flexichrome application with Marshall's Spray-Glass will also seal in the color and give it a glossy finish. After the print is dry (it takes only a few minutes), one may proceed to add more dye. The procedure can be repeated several times if necessary.

Unorthodox as it may sound, I have often combined the application of Flexichrome colors and Marshall's extra-strong (transparent) oil colors. The choice of colors in the extra-strong colors allows one to work with them in the previously stated manner, with a swab or tuft application.

A similar or even better effect is achieved without having to mix the Flexichrome colors by rubbing over the print surface. In the case of mixing Flexichrome with oil colors, it is preferable to do the Flexichrome tints *first* and then add the oil colors to other parts (Plate 6). Also, one can apply Spray-Glass on the print, let it dry thoroughly, and then proceed to add extra-strong Marshall oil colors. The effects are astounding. One word of caution: be sure to follow the directions for spraying on the bottle label. If spraying is not done well a pebbly effect will spoil the smooth surface. Before setting the colors with steam or spray, make sure that all cleaning and corrections are right. Once the setting or spraying is done it is difficult and harmful to the surface to remove paint. However, one can repeat various corrections on the *second* application, though it was pre-sprayed, without affecting the previous layer.

Oil Coloring Method

The colorist who thinks he will soon be out of business because of the terrific popularity of color photography will certainly rejoice to learn that he is more in business than ever. The clever colorist can apply his coloring techniques and color sense to retouching or spotting color prints of any make.

For anyone interested in pursuing color retouching I strongly suggest learning the basic steps of photo-oil coloring from my book *Hand Coloring Your Photographs With Oil and Dyes.* Since this chapter is not a lesson in oil coloring techniques but only pertains to the procedure of applying them to color prints, we shall proceed with the actual technique.

PROCEDURE

1. First evaluate the corrections you wish to perform with dyes on the print. Spotting out small areas of strong highlights, touching up lips and eyebrows, filling in stray hairs, subduing blemishes by stippling a darker flesh tone around skin area—all these corrections should be done *before* oil coloring. It does not matter if one retouches a portrait, puts color spots on flowers, leaves on a landscape, or accentuates separation between one or the other color—the detail is done with dye on the unsprayed surface.

2. When all dye corrections have been made, the print must be dry for a spraying with Marshall's Pre-Color Spray or Kodak's matte lacquer. Let it dry thoroughly (it takes only a few minutes) and then proceed with the application of Marshall's oil colors. If you want to change the background to an entirely different shade, mix Titanium or Zinc White with any color to make the background opaque and cover it. The same is useful for changing the color of a dress or a sky, removing a pole from a picture, a building, or any other unwanted object. (See Color Plates 10 and 11.)

The oil color is applied with a cotton-tipped skewer (as in previous methods) or with a small tuft of cotton for large areas. At all times the touch should be light and rotary, softly blending one area after another without streaks or blotches. The smaller the area, the tinier the rotating stroke. After the picture is finished, one can still apply the color pencil to parts to be corrected. If the pencil does not take readily, spray the print again with Pre-Color Spray and apply retouching pencils where necessary. The choice is yours as to whether you wish to have the final surface glossy or matte. In other words, the lacquers determine the final surface effect, and one may use matte and glossy lacquer, one over the other. However, for working with oil colors, the *print must be sprayed matte first* before it will accept opaque oil colors. Only when extra-strong colors are used and the surface is buffed for a glossy finish is before-and-after spraying unnecessary.

The extra-strong oil colors are very useful for enhancing backgrounds or landscapes. Color prints for reproduction will gain particularly by this method. Also, Polaroid Land prints may be worked and improved by the use of oil colors. If flesh tones are very pale, as is usually the case with prints made from color slides or film, a touch of Marshall's flesh color will be a great improvement. The application of the various print lacquers that have appeared lately on the market are a great advantage to the colorist, who in previous years had to treat the glossy surface with sizing medium in order to get anything accomplished.

The scope of correcting and improving color photography is limited only by the retoucher's imagination and skill. Pale and faded color prints can be renewed with this method. This "rejuvenating" of color prints is of great value to the photographer who has a stack of prints that have been exposed for some time in the show window. Faded from the strong daylight, they are of no use to him. However, after certain changes and additions of color have been performed, he has a brand-new supply of samples to show his customers.

REMOVING OIL COLOR

To correct or remove color, use only Marshall's Extender or Marlene. (They come with the regular coloring set.) Marlene will *completely remove color and spray,* whereas Extender removes *only the color.* Marlene should not be used on a Polaroid print. The proper instructions on how to use the Pre-Color Spray are indicated on the label of this product.

For a final finish use Pro-Tek-To spray for a matte surface and Spray-Glass for a glossier effect. Lacquers will keep the colors indefinitely fresh-looking, and since all color dyes (not oils) eventually fade, the lacquer spray will help preserve any color print.

Lacquer Over Color Prints

There are so many new ways to finish prints with lacquer sprays that it is suggested you write to the manufacturers (listed in the back of this book) for instruction booklets. Only the use of lacquer as it pertains to the corrective work was mentioned previously.

The corrective methods for improving color photography are limited only by the retoucher's imagination. Prints that faded from the sun in the studio window can be "rejuvenated," prints that were rejected because of spots or pale flesh tones can be made saleable or put on display, and the dreaded task of color print retouching can become an interesting challenge and a money-saver to boot.

CHAPTER 13

Conclusion

In this book I have tried to explain every possible technique I have been using through the years, yet I am sure the reader will discover some product or procedure that has not been mentioned. I must admit that to explain visual art, which retouching by all means is, one is confronted with the gap between the written word and the actual demonstration of a technique.

That is the reason why I decline to give full homestudy courses to a novice. Maybe writing or home repairs can be taught successfully by "remote control," but unfortunately professional retouching, and by that I mean *really good* retouching, must be acquired by personal supervision. The advertised correspondence courses in retouching cost money and time and never fulfill what they promised. You might just as well get a good book and start experimenting on your own.

The beginner should try to get in touch with a photo studio that might recommend a good retoucher, or even find a studio owner who would train him as an apprentice. (That's the way I learned it.) Large studios and laboratories throughout the states train retouchers for eventual employment. Also, photography schools advertise "crash courses" that last a week or two. They won't make a retoucher out of you in a week, but at least you will know what to do to improve your work.

Finally, I must mention the National Retouchers Guild, which I founded in 1966. It is the first such organization that exists solely for the benefit of its members and is dedicated to giving them assistance and advice in their work.

The greatest problem for the beginner is to acquire a supply of practice negatives and prints, and also to find a good source of practical retouching equipment. The NRG offers this unique service. If you can't get the supplies mentioned in this book, write to the NRG for information. If you need color negatives or black-and-white studio negatives and prints, order them from the NRG. Ten color negatives of various sizes with color proofs and directions on color negative retouching are supplied for $6.00 (including postage and handling). Order from: National Retouchers Guild, P.O. Box 535, Santa Barbara, Calif. 93102, or write for information about the advantages of membership. Professional or student members get negatives and evaluation free. The yearly dues for professional members is $12.00, for student members (one free lesson) it is $15.00. To each member I give my personal attention and try to assist the best way I can.

I am of the firm conviction that a person who has shown self-discipline and determination by acquiring the equipment and using some suggestions in this book will not lack the inspiration that will make him a capable worker in this fascinating and lucrative profession.

LIST OF SUPPLIERS

Dale Color Inc.
P.O. Box 460
Bloomington, Ill. 61701

Eastman Kodak Company
Rochester, N.Y. 14650

Jamieson Products Company
9341 Peninsula Dr.
Dallas, Texas 75218

John G. Marshall Mfg. Co., Inc.
167 N. Ninth Street
Brooklyn, N.Y. 11

McDonald Photo Products, Inc.
P.O. Box 22224
Dallas, Texas 75222

National Retouchers Guild
P.O. Box 535
Santa Barabara, Calif. 93102

The Pierce Co.
3701 Nicollet Ave.
Minneapolis, Minn. 55409

Retouch Methods Co., Inc.
P.O. Box 345
Chatham, N.J. 07928

Index

Index

E

F

G

H

I

J

K

R

S